CRISTOFORO COLOMBO
GOD'S NAVIGATOR

CRISTOFORO COLOMBO

GOD'S NAVIGATOR

DOUGLAS T. PECK

Columbian Publishers
A Division of the Columbus Museum
Columbus, Wisconsin

CRISTOFORO COLOMBO
GOD'S NAVIGATOR

Copyright 1993 by Douglas T. Peck

Published by:
Columbian Publishers
A Division of the Columbus Museum
Columbus, Wisconsin 53925-0151

ISBN 0-9641798-0-6
Library of Congress Catalog Card No. 94-72094

This book has been adapted from *An Empirical Reconstruction of Columbus'
Discovery Voyage in 1492 and His Return Voyage in 1493*, privately published,
copyrighted and given limited distribution by the author in 1991. Portions
of the author's "Ricostruzione e Analisi del Diario di Colombo del 1492,"
Columbus 92, Genoa Italy, 1991 and "Gooney Bird" Seeks Columbus Landfall,
South Florida History, Miami FL, 1992, have been adapted from these
publications and reprinted with their permission. Data and material on the
Ponce de León voyage in Chapter 7 are taken from the author's previously
published book; *Ponce de León and the Discovery of Florida*,
Pogo Press, Inc., St. Paul MN, 1993, with copyright permission granted.

FRONT COVER DESIGN AND ART by the author.

BACK COVER PHOTOGRAPH by Chris Mikula,
The Bradenton Herald, Bradenton, Florida.

Figures 8 & 10 are original art by George Prout. All other
illustrative drawings and charts are original art and drafting
by the author except as noted in the List of Illustrations.

Dedication

To my wife Becky.
Her vital and supportive role in keeping my family and business affairs running smoothly at home during my six and seven month long research voyages was a very real part of the total effort which produced this book

Contents

DOUGLAS T. PECK
Bradenton, Florida

COLUMBIAN PUBLISHERS
A Division of the Columbus Museum
Columbus, WI 53925-0151

Acknowledgements

I must start by acknowledging my good friends and fellow Columbian scholars in the Phileas Society who were the first to encourage me to use my navigational background and expertise in a serious historical research program on the Columbus voyage. These include Robert Tolf, Fred Ruffner, Dan and Rose Amato, Thornton Thomas, Joseph Laufer, Admiral William Lemos, Julian Granberry, and the late Robert Power. Their sincere support and encouragement which started in a Columbus seminar in Palos, Spain, in 1987 was not a one time thing and has continued to this day.

My several research voyages which both started and terminated in the Huelva-Palos area was assured of a successful completion by the grateful and freely given assistance I received from my good friends in Spain; Manuel Iglesias Fernandez Director of the Huelva Turismo Office, Juan Ortiz Garcia Presidente of the Club Maritimo de Huelva, and of course the Mayor of Palos and member of the Spanish Parliament, Alcaldesa Pilar Bulgar Fraile.

Then I must acknowledge the vital role my colleagues in the Society for the History of Discoveries played in the preparation of this book. Their expertise in the discipline of historical research was unselfishly shared with me in my sometimes agonizing transition from an ocean navigator to research historian. Included in this group of erudite scholars are John Parker, David Buisseret, James Kelley, Oliver Dunn, David Henige, Helen Wallis, Donald McGuirk, Gregory McIntosh, Neil Sealey, and Donald Gerace.

Jim Kelley deserves special recognition for his unselfish, and I am sure time consuming assistance in furnishing me his analytical interpretation of some of the obscure or ambiguous navigational data contained in the Columbus log. And he certainly has the credentials for this task as he is the co-author (with Oliver Dunn) of the latest and most widely accepted definitive translation of the Las Casas Columbus log published as, *The Diario of Christopher Columbus's First Voyage to America*. Kelley was also instrumental in the basic academic research for my earlier book, *Ponce de León and the Discovery of Florida*. Portions of that book have applied to this text and used in Chapter 7.

I met Paolo Emilio Taviani on San Salvador, Bahamas in 1989 when he was there to dedicate the newly opened Columbus Museum on the island. Dr. Taviani is the Dean of the Italian Parliament, Senator for Life, and a world renowned Columbian historian and author. We had a long talk about my research voyage during which I was gratified (overwhelmed would be a better word) to learn that he knew of and admired my work and asked permission to translate my paper into Italian for publication in Italy. Since that time we have carried on a lively correspondence and his encouragement to me on my research voyages has been of inestimable value. I consider it a signal honor that he wrote the Foreword for this book.

Dr. Helen Wallis also deserves special recognition for her valuable assistance in my (1988) search in the cartographical library of the British Museum in London for 16th century documents relating to the Columbus voyage. Dr. Wallace had just retired as Director of the cartographical library and I would never have gotten through those two locked and guarded doors without her. Helen spent an entire day with me digging out much valuable data on reports of early 16th century magnetic variation, but the highlight was when she found the galley proofs of the 1542 Jean Rotz map (used in Chapter 7) in the archives and was able to make me a full sized copy.

My next acknowledgement is a bit unusual in that it must be to an entire city and the civic leaders of that community. My grateful thanks must go to Dan Amato, President, 1992 Columbus Quincentennial Celebration, Inc., and to Knights of Columbus, Columbus Council #1609, and to my many friends in Columbus Wisconsin, who with unselfish dedication gave me both monetary assistance and much needed encouragement, which was of inestimable help in accomplishing the long and arduous research voyages resulting in this book.

My research for the book involved the use of my sailing yacht "Gooney Bird" in long and specialized voyages, the preparation for which required technical advice and assistance from the many friends involved in my sailing enterprises. They are too numerous to mention but they know who they are and to them I extend my heartfelt thanks and wish them "Fair Winds."

My son Douglas W. Peck also played a vital role in the production of the manuscript. My computer and word processor is definitely not user-friendly and I found it would constantly refuse to follow my instructions, even talking back to me in a derogatory manner. In this I am blessed with the fact that Douglas is a business education teacher and an expert on computers, so he was able to solve my problems quickly and easily, allowing me to complete the book within sometimes formidable deadlines.

Foreword

What, in our century, has been offered to us by the academic Columbian historical record, that is new or on a truly scientific plane?

There have been only a few new findings in this century of a valid documentary nature: The Assereto document (Genoa 1904); The Piri Reis map (Istanbul 1929); The Copiador book (Spain 1985). These have only modified, and even then in the most modest detail, that which already was known (by the time of the fourth centennial) of Christopher Columbus and his feat of discovery.

The truly great and significant new findings of this century stem from studies of the geographical, navigational, and maritime documents of the great Genoese navigator. *Douglas T. Peck's book is just such a study.*

These studies were initiated by Samuel Eliot Morison; his work was fundamental, next to that of Cesare De Lollis, and he was assisted by a dear friend and scholar, Mauricio Obregon, rector of the University of Bogota. I have dedicated part of my life to finishing Morison's work, extending and clarifying the period preceding the discovery.

I am duty-bound to maintain my just claim as a historian and geographer; I am not, However, an experienced seaman and navigator. This book, following the research by Morison and myself, is the first valid and scientifically sound historical study of both the navigation expertise of Columbus, and the track of his voyage from Gomera to his landfall, accomplished by an experienced seaman and navigator.

Peck is the first to have accomplished a scientifically controlled research voyage duplicating the track across the Atlantic by following the navigational data in Columbus' log. He is the first qualified navigator to have completed detailed field studies of the pertinent historical sites, not only their geography in general, but most importantly the geography of a maritime nature, as related to identifying the landfall from the data in Columbus' navigator's log. His in-depth research focused not only on the track across the Atlantic but on other areas of the seas which were involved in the study of Columbus' voyage, to include San Salvador, Rum Cay, Long Island, Crooked-Acklins Island, Fortune Island, Samana Cay, and others.

Douglas Peck's concrete and substantiated conclusions are very significant in that they not only eliminate Egg Island, Caicos and Turks Islands, and other lesser landfall proposals, but completely demolish the hypothesis of Robert Fuson and Joseph Judge in supporting the National Geographic Society's proposal that the landfall of Columbus was on Samana Cay.

The work by Peck is not only opportune but meets a compelling need to correct the distorted views on Columbus' navigation and to confirm with definite authority that Columbus' landfall was the island the native Indians called "Guanahani", which later acquired the name of Watling, and then justly, in 1926, was renamed San Salvador by the governor of the Bahamas.

This book should be a required addition in European and American libraries if they are to adequately and factually cover the history of the Columbian era.

Paolo Emilio Taviani

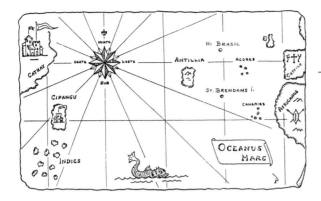

Introduction

"An age will come after many years when the ocean will loose the chains of things and a huge land lie revealed; when Jason's pilot Tethy's will disclose New Worlds and Thule no more be the ultimate."

From Seneca's *Medea*, 45 AD

"This prophecy was fulfilled by my father the Admiral in the year 1492."

Annotation in Columbus' copy of *Medea*, by his son Ferdinand Colon

I live in two worlds. I am both an avidly active ocean sailor and navigator, and at the same time a dedicated academic student of history. These two seemingly unrelated attributes came together in 1985 when I embarked on a detailed study of the discovery voyage of Columbus with emphasis on his ocean navigation. My initial goal was to answer two questions that have been perplexing historians down through the centuries. These can be simply stated: Was Columbus really an expert navigator? And which of the many islands in the Bahamas was his landfall in the New World?

The fundamental training, knowledge, and expertise of Columbus as a deep sea navigator has been a subject of controversy from the time of his appearances before the courts of Portugal and Spain to the present time. Down through the ages Columbus has been pictured as either a seafaring genius, far ahead of his time in the science of navigation, or as an unschooled opportunist and adventurer with little seafaring and navigation experience, who accomplished his mission only by sheer luck and with the help of other more experienced participants.

The many biographers seem to be about evenly divided on this question. Humbolt, Morison, and Taviani call him a seafaring genius, while Harisse, Vignaud, and Varnhagen picture him as a simple wool weaver whose primary attributes were a vivid imagination and a charismatic manner which allowed him to sell himself as a cosmographer and navigator. Who's right here? What's the answer?

The log or "diario" of the 1492 discovery voyage and the 1493 return voyage of Columbus as summarized by Fray Bartolomè de Las Casas is equally controversial. One school of thought views it as a reasonably accurate navigational log which can be analyzed and studied to determine the actual track of Columbus as well as determine his accuracy and expertise in navigation. The other school considers the log so full of errors and anomalies as to be relatively worthless as a research document to determine his track and pinpoint the true landfall island. Again, who's right? What's the answer?

While conducting my initial research on the navigation of Columbus I soon realized there were many other controversial questions about Columbus and his voyages that beg an answer. Questions such as: What was the real (not the popular) purpose of the voyage? Was Columbus interested only in titles and material gain or did he have a higher goal? How did his contract with the sovereigns of Spain read, and did he carry it out or did he fail?

Some of these more mundane questions as well as the technical questions of Columbus' navigation and landfall have been addressed by a spate of opportunist historians who have published a plethora of books spurred on by the fleeting public interest in the Columbus Quincentennial Celebration. For the most part these books (I have provided only the most important ones in my bibliography) raise and discuss the questions but seldom provide the factual or historically correct answers. This book provides the answers in the thoroughly researched and documented thesis following.

My research in this discipline was begun early in 1985 with the limited goal of determining the expertise of Columbus as a navigator and pinpointing his landfall in the Bahamas by analysis of his log. At the end of a carefully logged 34 day voyage from Gomera, Columbus made landfall on a small island in the Bahamas which he described in some detail and reported the Taino Indians called it Guanahani. At first glance it would seem a simple enough task to follow that log and find the island that answered the description and bore the Indian name. But such has not been the case, and for centuries leading scholars from around the world have been in disagreement as to just which island in the Bahamas is Guanahani, the true landfall of Columbus.

To prove the case for a particular island, previous historians had taken Columbus' log and artificially plotted his course across the Atlantic to his landfall on Guanahani. I resolved instead to use my deep draft sea going cutter "Gooney Bird" to re-sail the daily compass headings and distances provided by his log and thus determine his track and locate his landfall island of Guanahani.

This empirical research methodology of using a sailboat as a test vehicle in reconstruction of the voyage from the log is new to this particular field of historical research. In this regard, I have found that the ultra-conservative academic community is reluctant to accept anything new, and particularly a concept in which they lack the technical training and expertise to understand. This empirical research methodology is fully explained in Chapter 4.

Following my research and preliminary voyage in 1985, the *National Geographic* magazine in their November 1986 issue carried a comprehensive article on the Columbus landfall in which they determined that Columbus' landfall island of Guanahani was in fact Samana Cay in the Bahamas. Luis Marden who had plotted (using a computer) Columbus' track across the Atlantic to Samana Cay had this to say at the end of the article: "It remains now for a sailing vessel to take a departure from the Canaries in September and to steer Columbus' courses by compass alone, due west where he went due west and elsewhere where he deviated, and see where it ends up."

That did it! That was my needed encouragement which convinced me that my planned use of a sailing vessel to re-sail the log, rather than use of artificial plotting on a chart, was a viable form of empirical testing and research to reconstruct the track of Columbus to his landfall. Indeed, the reader will learn in chapters 5 & 6 that the use of a sailing vessel using actual empirical sea conditions provides far superior research data than a computer with suspect or erroneous sea conditions programmed into it.

In 1987 I performed my first controlled research voyage in "Gooney Bird" following Columbus' log from Gomera to his landfall in the New World. I found that Columbus' log led me to the island of San Salvador in the Bahamas rather than Samana Cay as theorized by the National Geographic Society. Following this and with further research on the geographical features of Guanahani and the track through the islands to Cuba, I confirmed my finding of San Salvador as the true landfall of Columbus.

During 1988 my research thesis on the landfall was presented in formal lectures to leading historical societies across the country and to the Royal Geographical Society in London. Then in 1989 my thesis was translated into Italian and published in a leading historical journal in Genoa, Italy.

However, while my thesis that San Salvador is the landfall island was well received both here and abroad, I found that it is very difficult indeed to tell the National Geographic Society that they are wrong!

Seeking further proof, I then (1990) re-sailed and reconstructed Ponce de León's 1513 voyage from his log in the same manner that I did Columbus' voyage. Ponce de León in his voyage from Puerto Rico to the shores of Florida sailed up the chain of the Bahama islands and landed on an island which his Indian guides identified as Guanahani, the landfall island of Columbus. My research thesis on this reconstruction published in the *Florida Historical Quarterly* firmly established San Salvador as the landfall island that Ponce de León identified and shows Samana Cay as located a full day's sail south-southeast of the true landfall.

My next research voyage was in 1991 when I re-sailed and reconstructed both the 1492 discovery voyage from Gomera to Guanahani and the return voyage from Hispaniola to Santa Maria, Azores. In this voyage (Chapters 5 & 6) I was able to fully document the navigational expertise of Columbus and the accuracy of his log, and once again confirmed San Salvador as the landfall island.

My academic research papers are liberally sprinkled with footnotes to substantiate or document key or controversial points. I have elected in this book to include the footnotes in the body of the text and then only in the most important or controversial items. I have also condensed and summarized the mass of technical navigation data which is necessary in an academic thesis to prove a point to a sometimes skeptical and critical audience. (As an example, the appendix to my original research paper listed 260 latitude/longitude fixes in the track!) But let me assure the reader that all conclusions in this book are based on hard cold mathematically proven facts rather than unsubstantiated speculation or conjecture.

Columbus while intent on his navigation and completion of his voyage still had time to sprinkle his log with observations that clearly showed he loved sailing and the sea for their own sake and not merely as the means to an end. In this I find that Columbus and I are kindred spirits and so have included some quasi-biographical material in the text to compare his 15th century experiences in sailing the "Santa Maria" across the ocean to the New World with my 20th century experiences in sailing "Gooney Bird" across that same ocean to learn how he did it.

Read on and you will find many new insights on Columbus and his voyage that are contained in no other book but this.

1

Columbus the Man

In my introduction I brought out the fact that biographers and historians are in disagreement over Columbus' navigation expertise. I found also that these same biographers and historians widely disagree on the character, personality, and family heritage of Columbus as a person. It is beyond the scope of this book to enter into this argument with a detailed and subjective thesis as I will do later in my treatment of the navigational questions. However, the two subjects of Columbus the Man, and Columbus the Navigator, are so intertwined and interrelated that the latter cannot be fully understood and appreciated without having a firm grasp on the former.

In my study of the many widely divergent biographical views of Columbus the Man, it soon became apparent that the series of biographies by Paolo Emilio Taviani stood head and shoulders above the rest for thoroughly documented historical truth. Accordingly this brief picture of Columbus the Man will be taken largely from Dr. Taviani's works.

It was inevitable that from the larger than life stature of Columbus would come the many claims by diverse communities and ethnic groups that he evolved from their heritage. Over the years there has appeared on the scene a Greek, English, Irish, Viking, Spanish, French, and Portuguese Columbus. Of these the French and the Portuguese produced three separate Columbuses and quite understandable in Spain both Castile and Catalonia have claimed the honor of being the birth place of Columbus.

It is significant that none of the many published and extant documents of historians and annalists in the 15th and 16th century questioned the fact that Columbus was born and spent his early life as a native of Genoa. Taviani has named 31 of the outstanding European historians of the 16th century,

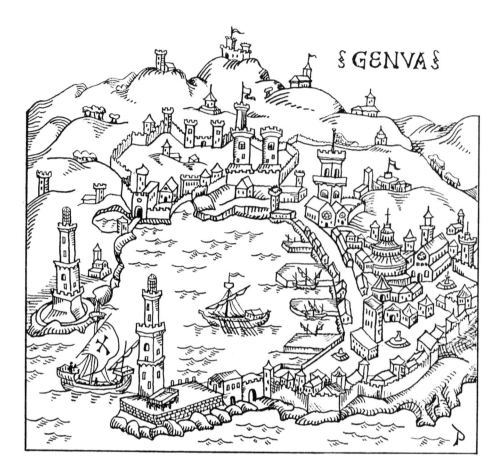

Figure 1. Genoa from a 16th century woodcut in Schedel's *Liber Chronicarum*, 1493.

beginning with Martyr, Las Casas, and Oviedo, and ending with Gomara, and Bernaldez, who affirm that Columbus was from the environs of Genoa. Not until the 18th and 19th and even continuing into the 20th century were these contrary, unfounded, and spurious claims put forward. Madariaga and Wassermann with their theory that Columbus was a Sephardic Jew from Catalan (Spain) are the scholars most often cited to disprove the Genoese heritage, but their fairly recent claims are founded on nebulous speculation rather than on documented facts.

Columbus' immediate family can be traced back to his grandfather Giovanni Colombo, then to his father Domenico Colombo and his mother Susanna Fontanarossa. His father was a master weaver who owned his own looms and bought the raw wool and wove it into cloth in what should have been a substantial if not wealthy business endeavor. He also dabbled in the wine and cheese business and entered into politics of the time usually on the losing side. A profusion of extant archival records generated by these endeavors indicate without equivocation that Domenico and his family were established Genoese citizens. Well over 100 of these authenticated 15th century documents are translated, recorded, and analyzed in the recent writings of Taviani, Farina, and Tolf (see Bibliography).

There is ample documentary evidence to show that all family members were firmly and devoutly attached to the Catholic faith yet there are some historians who claim that the family were "converso" (or secret) members of the Jewish faith. This unfounded claim is only supported by distorted and invalid conclusions based on some of the irrelevant and misinterpreted statements and actions of Columbus, and from the fact that some family names could be traced to the Old Testament. The fact that his mother's first name was Susanna (Susan) and her father was named Jacobo (Jacob) has been used in a strained hypothesis by some historians to indicate that the family was of Jewish blood. That same unreal reasoning could be applied to falsely indicate that the majority of gentile Christian families are Jewish since the Old Testament was then, and is now the most popular source for first names among Christians.

There may very well have been some Jewish blood in the dim and distant past of Columbus' family as there was in many European families of the time. But the point is we are dealing only with Columbus the man and we will see shortly that he was not only a devout follower but was an inspired leader in the Catholic faith.

The family were neither peasants or nobility, but were firmly entrenched in the rising middle class or merchant class whose authority and prestige was gaining steadily in early renaissance Europe. Columbus earned his nobility by his deeds, but his son Ferdinand in writing the biography of his father muddied the water by trying vainly to trace the family heritage to some ancient and nebulous nobility. At least Ferdinand ended his convoluted argument for inherited nobility by stating truthfully: "... But this is of no importance, since the family of Christopher Columbus begins with the man himself, sent by Providence to discover the New World."

Columbus was in every sense a self made man. From a modest beginning and education, he rapidly worked himself up to a point when only 24 years of age he was an accomplished and sought after sea captain in demand by many of the leading merchants and princes of the Mediterranean area. Many historians (including Morison) have promulgated the erroneous impression that Columbus was unschooled and illiterate into early manhood. This hardly squares with the fact that Ferdinand in the biography of his father states that:

"He learned his letters at a tender age." And Las Casas reports: "As a child his parents made him learn to read and write. ... He also studied arithmetic and drawing (cartography) with the same skill and degree of excellence."

Later in Portugal through dedicated study he was to become fluent in Portuguese, Castilian Spanish, and Latin, in addition to his native Italian languages. If he could only have been given an intelligence test at the time, he would undoubtedly have scored in the gifted or genius class.

His physical appearance and strong character traits were from his northern Italian Gothic (rather than Latin) ancestors. For a description of his physical appearance and personality I can rely with confidence on his contemporary, Bartolomé de Las Casas who wrote in his "Historia de las Indias": "He was more than middling tall; face long and giving an air of authority; aquiline nose, blue eyes, complexion light and tending to bright red; beard and hair red when young but very soon turned gray from his labors; he was affable and cheerful in speaking, and eloquent and boastful in his negotiations; he was serious in moderation, affable with strangers, and with members of his household gentle and pleasant, with modest gravity and discreet conversation; and so could easily incite those who saw him to love him. In fine, he was most impressive in his port and countenance. He was sober and moderate in eating, drinking, clothing and footwear; it was commonly said that he spoke cheerfully in familiar conversation, or with indignation when he gave reproof or was angry with somebody. In matters of the Christian religion, without doubt he was a Catholic and of great devotion; for in everything he did or said or sought to begin, he always interposed 'In the name of the Holy Trinity I will do this.' In whatever letter or other thing he wrote, he put at the head 'Jesus and Mary be with us on the way,' and of these writings in his own hand I have plenty now in my possession. He was extraordinarily zealous for the divine service; he desired and was eager for the conversion of these people (the Indians), and that in every region the faith of Jesus Christ be planted and enhanced."

This is how Columbus appeared to those who knew him for a long period of his life and therefore is more accurate than those distorted versions we get from some historians of a much later date.

From the media attention given to Columbus during the recent Quincentennial Celebration of his epic voyage we can only conclude he is the victim of a "bad press." He has been unmercifully blamed for the mistreatment, torturing, enslavement, and genocide of the Indian population. This is like blaming the physician for the cancer and wrongfully presumes that this was Columbus' intention and if he had only stayed home none of this would have happened.

A comprehensive review of how this media view of Columbus has changed dramatically down through the years is contained in Benjamin Keen's Introduction to his book *Admiral Christopher Columbus*, published by Rutgers University Press. In this we find that the publications attending the 1892-3 "World's Columbian Exposition" lauded Columbus as a heroic, virtuous, and nearly Divine figure, with serious attempts to change the nomenclature of America and American to Columbia and Columbian. This change to the "bad press" of Columbus in the 1992 Quincentennial Celebration can easily be attributed to the idyllic peace and prosperity of the New World in 1892, compared to the chaotic wars, revolutions, depressions, and human rights violations of the current century. It is truly mind boggling to see how well known writers can review the same documents containing the history of Columbus' voyages, and then come up with such widely divergent views concerning Columbus' responsibility for these widespread human rights violations.

There is ample documentary evidence to show that Columbus' primary interest *in the Indians* was their conversion to the Christian religion, and their enslavement and subsequent mistreatment was brought about by circumstances entirely beyond his control. Las Casas in reporting the "palabras formales" (exact words) of Columbus on the first day of the landing quotes him as saying: "In order that we might win good friendship, because I knew that they were a people who could better be freed and *converted to our Holy Faith* by love than by force,..."

In this instance we are speaking entirely of the gentle Taino Indians in the islands and on Española (Hispaniola) as Columbus at a later date in referring to the cannibalistic Caribs had this to say: "I will also bring ... many slaves who will be taken only from the idolaters (Caribs)." This statement which seems to contradict my previous assertion that Columbus was interested primarily in conversion of the Indians to Christianity must be taken in the context of the 15th century Church dogma and policy toward idolaters (such as cannibals) for which Columbus can hardly be held accountable.

The military commanders Alonzo de Hojeda and Mosén Pedro Margarit were the first to cruelly mistreat the Taino Indians in their 1494 campaigns into the interior of Española in search of gold. Columbus had explicitly told both men to treat the Indians kindly and had reminded them that; "Their Highnesses desire more the salvation of these people (the Indians) by making them Christians, than all the riches that can be obtained from them."

In this instance Columbus was quoting from the formal charter issued by the crown for his second voyage to the newly discovered "Indies." This formal charter was issued in Barcelona on 29 May, 1493 and declared that "the *prime*

Figure 2. Columbus protecting the Indians from the cruelty of the Spanish colonists in an 1878 etching by Leopold Flameng.

object of the voyage was the conversion of the natives." The Benedictine monk Fray Bernal Buil with a contingent of "religiosos" was sent to carry out this part of the mission but was soon overwhelmed by events.

The charter then goes on to state that the *second* object of the voyage was to establish a crown trading colony and carry on further exploration. To follow this up, in a log entry on 5 December 1492, Columbus further confirmed the *primary* purpose of the enterprise when he stated: "And I say that your highnesses (Ferdinand and Isabela) ought not to consent that any foreigner do business or set foot here, except Christian Catholics, since this was the *end and the beginning* of the enterprise, that it should be for the *enhancement and glory of the Christian Religion*, nor should anyone who is not a good Christian come to these parts."

Columbus was a seaman and navigator and not a military commander or administrative governor so he was hard put to convince the Spanish colonists that the salvation of the Indians should come ahead of their quest for gold. He was viewed by the Spaniards as a hated foreign interloper, and soon lost control of the first colonies on Española. While the mission of the first colony in America was conceived of as first converting the natives to Christianity then acquiring gold, the first and higher goal was soon submerged by the latter. Las Casas stated Columbus' problem very succinctly when he noted that the Spanish colonists were so surly, belligerent, and crazed for gold that "even the Archangel Gabriel could not have governed them."

Columbus was a keen observer and noted and reported on the geographical features of the land and the surrounding sea at all the places he visited, as he was to do later in his log. He had the searching, inquisitive mind of the born innovator and explorer, which explains why he signed on a British vessel out of Bristol to Iceland just to see that end of the world. It was this same trait, or more properly drive, that compelled him to sail west across the unknown sea to the New World. But here we must ask if it was solely this personality trait or drive that motivated Columbus to his great adventure?

Columbus was driven by an overwhelming obsession to find a westward route to the Indies. Was it just finding the route and proving that he was right that was an end in itself? Was it the gold and spices that would make Spain (and himself) richer? What was his real underlying motivation?

The historical truth that Columbus in seeking the westward route to the Indies was primarily interested in bringing Christianity to that part of the world has been completely overshadowed and pushed out of the picture by the emphasis placed on his concurrently seeking gold, spices, and unfortunately slaves to further that mission. This is not to say that *as a navigator* his ultimate goal (which he had to prove) was primarily to find the westward route to the Indies. But here we are discussing Columbus the man, and will cover his navigational goals and achievements in the ensuing chapters.

It is beyond the scope of this study to get into the complicated discussion of how this singular mission got so out of hand (covered to excess by myriad historians) so I have limited my discussion to just documenting the true purpose of Columbus' "Enterprise of the Indies" *as he perceived it*. And let me emphasize here that this was not how Ferdinand, or the court, or the Spanish ship owners and sailors, or later historians, or anyone else, saw or perceived the purpose of the enterprise. This is solely how *Columbus the man perceived it*.

Figure 3. Copy of the insert on Juan de la Cosa's map showing Columbus as St. Christopher carrying the Christ Child to the New World.

I have shown in my previous quotes from Columbus' journal that both he and the Spanish sovereigns (with Isabela being the strongest) were primarily interested in bringing Christianity to the New World. There are numerous other similar instances to support this view that I could cite from Columbus' journals and letters, but the best examples are contained in his "Book of Prophecies" which he wrote late in his life during the year 1501, only five years before his death.

Most historians put Columbus' "Book of Prophecies" down as just the incoherent ranting and railing of a senile and disillusioned old man. This false impression is probably brought about by Columbus' allegorical style of writing in the book, which actually only follows the style of most 16th century writings by Church clerics. Like these Church clerics he bases his argument on both quotes from the scriptures and quotes from learned and accepted theologians of the time, rather than on direct but unsupported assertion.

Kay Brigham in her excellent analysis of the "Book of Prophecies" (see bibliography) brings out the fact that this is Columbus' completely lucid and documented thesis to show that the fundamental objective of his "Enterprise of the Indies" was the cause of furthering Christianity. The discovery of the route to the Indies and the gold it brought was thus to serve only as a medium of exchange to defend and further Christian values in Spain, the Mediterranean, the Holy Land, and the Indies.

Columbus in his "mayorazqo" or will dated 22 February, 1498, specified that a church and hospital were to be erected in Española and maintained with "four good Masters of Sacred Theology whose main object shall be to work for the conversion of the natives." Columbus' wishes as to the church were carried out by his son Diego but sadly by the time the church was erected there were no Indians to convert.

Another graphic example of this theme is the insert on Juan de la Cosa's map of the New World (see Figure 3) in which Columbus is depicted as his namesake St. Christopher, carrying the Christ Child on his back to the New World. Juan de la Cosa was a shipmate of Columbus on his voyages so would be fully acquainted with Columbus' firmly held belief that he had a Divine mission to bring Christianity to the Indies.

It is interesting to note that Juan de la Cosa depicts a bearded Columbus while most other portraits of Columbus show him clean shaven. Most sailors of the time were clean shaven when ashore in Spain but would let their beards grow at sea where shaving facilities (primarily water) were scarce or non-existent. Here we must remember that Juan de la Cosa knew Columbus at sea rather than ashore so this is quite probably a true depiction of what Columbus looked like on his voyages.

Figure 4. Columbus being greeted in state on his triumphant return from the Indies as pictured in the 1878 French biography by Marquis Belloy.

The high religious qualities of Columbus and his mission were later recognized by leaders of the Church who made an attempt to beatify him as a saint in the early decades of the 19th century. Count Roselly de Lorgues, Pope Pius IX, tried to initiate the process of canonization with the Roman Curia in 1865. This attempt was unsuccessful and very little is known of the proceedings as they were kept quite secret. The renowned Latin American author Alejo Carpentier, wrote a historical novel (only recently translated into English) based on this event. His novel is pure allegorical fiction but probably names the real reason for Columbus' rejection from sainthood as his failure to wed his mistress Beatriz Enriquez de Harana on the birth of their son Ferdinand.

I mentioned earlier that Columbus' nobility began with his 1492 discovery voyage and we find that the Christopher Columbus name and heritage has continued in Spain to this day.

Ferdinand Colon, Columbus' scholarly youngest son became a noted humanist, book collector (with one of the largest libraries in Europe) archivist for Columbus' papers, and correspondent of Erasmus. His family name ended with him as he died without issue.

Columbus' eldest son, Don Diego Colon, became governor of Española and inherited the titles of Admiral of the Ocean Sea and Duke of Veragua. Diego's only legitimate son, Don Luis Colon was a disgrace to the family but nevertheless retained the titles Admiral of the Indies (changed from the Ocean Sea) and Duke of Veragua, then later picked up the titles Marquess of Jamaica and Duke of Vega.

After Don Luis Colon the family name and heritage becomes complicated as it sometimes passed through daughters, picking up the mother's name in the Spanish tradition. During many successive generations the name and titles traveled to England then back to Spain where in 1940 it rested with Cristobal Colon de Carvajal y Maroto Hurtado de Mendoza y Perez del Pulgar, who retained the titles Duke of Veragua, Duke of Vega, Marquess of Jamaica, and Grand Admiral of the Indies. Sensibly his descendants when dealing with the American media now only use the shortened (and Anglicized) family name of Christopher Columbus.

It was Christopher Columbus XX and his son Christopher Columbus XXI who greeted Dan Amato, the President of the Columbus Wisconsin 1992 Columbus Quincentennial Celebration Commission, on his 1992 visit to Spain. Amato was in Spain to carry through an official USA Quincentenary Celebration Event of planting redwood trees from the New World on the shores of Spain in the Old World. It is indeed gratifying to see that the descendants of Columbus are still active in the civic life of Spain and carrying on the memory of his epic voyage and achievement.

This has been a study of Columbus the man, but it is as a navigator that Columbus is best known and in which he made his greatest impact on history. And it is the enigma and controversy over Columbus' navigation that is the main thrust of this book and will be thoroughly covered in the ensuing chapters.

2

Columbus the Navigator

Columbus began his seafaring and navigation training and experience at a very early age, probably between 12 and 14 years of age while living in the vicinity of Genoa. Ferdinand Colon, Columbus' youngest son gave us an insight into his father's seafaring experience when he wrote his *Historie*, a biography of his father. Written largely from memory and many years after Columbus' death, the book contains many distortions and inconsistencies, but it does give us information to show Columbus' wide experience as a seaman and navigator prior to 1492. In Chapter IV of the *Historie* Ferdinand quotes a letter from Columbus to the Spanish sovereigns which begins: "I went to sea very young, and have continued it to this day."

Columbus' father, Domenico Colombo, was a wool weaver so he no doubt would have attended the weaver's guild school as a child. Paolo Emilio Taviani in his comprehensive and superbly documented biography of Columbus, brings out the fact that the early renaissance guild schools in Italy gave a basic education that was far ahead of the schools in northern and western Europe. In coastal cities this education would include basic mathematics and skills related to seafaring and navigation.

At this time Columbus would have divided his time between working in his father's shop and going to sea as was the accepted custom of all young men of Genoa. The Genoese annalists Bartolomeo Senaraga and Antonio Gallo wrote of Christopher and Bartholomew Columbus that "having reached puberty, according to the custom of the people, they had begun to navigate."

Columbus left no chronological account of his voyages at sea so what we have must be gleaned from his remarks in his logs and letters, and from the biography by his son Ferdinand. It is understandable why there is no written record of Columbus' early life as a seafarer, for he had yet to become famous so there was no need to record the life of just another one of the many young Genoese seamen of the time. But from these later written sources we can put together the extensive and significant training and experience of Columbus which reveals him to be among the foremost and best qualified seamen and navigators in Europe prior to his epic voyage of 1492.

Genoa was one of the principal ports in medieval Europe with it's merchants sending their ships to range the Mediterranean gathering the products of the East and delivering them to the growing market in northern and western Europe. In this environment, Columbus was to rise rapidly from apprentice seaman to master and pilot (captain and navigator) when he was still a young man. The signal fact that Columbus' expertise as a navigator was derived from his Genoese heritage is what prompted me to use the Italian spelling of "Cristoforo Colombo" in the title of the book.

His reputation as an experienced and capable captain must have been known throughout the Mediterranean for in 1472 at the age of 23 or 24 he was commissioned by Rene d'Anjou to captain a corsair enterprise in Tunisian waters to capture the Aroganese ship Fernandina. Morison does Columbus a disservice at this point in asserting without foundation that: "No young fellow of about twenty who had been carding and weaving wool most of his life could so quickly have risen to command." Morison is off base here in picturing Columbus as only carding and weaving wool during the 9 or 10 year period (from age 14) when he was serving his apprenticeship as a seaman and navigator. And how is it that Morison is so surprised at Columbus quickly rising to command when as an official historian for the U.S.Navy he should have known that John Paul Jones (the Father of the American Navy) was only 22 when given his first command.

The report of this corsair mission from Columbus' son Ferdinand contains an apocryphal story about how Columbus reversed the compass needles to fool the crew, which may have come from the imagination of either Columbus or Ferdinand to try and prove some obscure point. This part of the report is pure nonsense, but the important point here is that he was hired to Captain the mission, and this fact could not have been fabricated since such prominent people and events were involved.

Through his close association with Paolo di Negro and Nicola Spinola, two of the leading ship owners of Genoa, Columbus would have had maximum opportunity to hone and perfect his navigational skills throughout the Mediterranean and beyond. This association was to last on through the years and at a later date Columbus was to remember the sons and heirs of Paolo di Negro and Nicola Spinola in his will.

In a letter of 1502 he indicates familiarity with the ports and shoreline of Naples, Marseilles, the islands of Hyeres, Cape Creus in Catalonia, the Bay of Narbonne, Sardinia, and the Barbary coast. In this same letter he gives complete sailing instructions for a course from Cadiz to Naples for both summer and winter months which amounted to a navigational rutter (navigator's guide) that could only have been gained from personal knowledge and experience.

You probably see by now that the picture of some historians that Columbus was just a bumbling wool weaver with limited experience at sea is completely false. But there is more!

In the Mediterranean he would have learned and perfected his basic skill in dead reckoning navigation. The term dead reckoning is derived from deductive (ded) reckoning, a form of navigation for determining position by plotting a given magnetic compass course for a given distance. These compass courses and distances were then plotted on a portolan chart so the pilot could fix his position in relation to his departure port or any other landmark on the chart. Notice I stated the compass *course* was plotted on the chart rather than the compass *heading*. The compass course may or may not be the same as the compass heading steered due to outside influences, primarily magnetic variation and ocean currents. This technical point which has a vital influence on interpretation and analysis of Columbus' navigation will be fully explained in Chapters 4, 5, & 6 following.

The portolan chart was a large bleached sheepskin upon which the 15th century pilot plotted his dead reckoning course. The portolan chart is sometimes referred to as a "port finding" chart from which the name derives. Entries were made with ink but the sheepskin could be scraped clean and used over and over again. (This fact may very well account for the disappearance of the early navigator's holograph charts.) And in some ways for a sailing vessel it was superior to our modern paper charts which disintegrate when wet.

The early Mediterranean pilot or navigator had no need for celestial navigation (which was then in it's infancy for practical marine use) since most of his passages were along a shoreline with only an occasional one or two day hop out of sight of land. I should perhaps clarify my remark about celestial navigation being in its infancy because the Vikings, Phoenicians and other ancient seafarers used the north star and the rising and setting sun to provide a primitive (and highly inaccurate) form of celestial navigation before the advent of the magnetic compass. The key wording here is *for practical marine use*.

This basic dead reckoning form of navigation was introduced into Europe with the advent of the practical marine compass in the 13th century and

Figure 5. The dead reckoning traverse board used to record compass course and distance during each watch. A separate board was used for each watch timed by the sand glass shown.

by the time of Columbus was perfected to the point that European navigators were making long overwater passages with accuracy and precision as will be shown in the text to follow.

Dead reckoning navigation requires that each change of course and each change of speed be recorded by the man at the helm so the pilot could plot the ship's position on a chart. The helmsman (or watch captain in charge) not only wouldn't have any paper for this record but was probably illiterate and unable to write it down if he had the writing materials. So a simple mechanical and visual presentation called a traverse board was used for this task. The traverse board provided pegs with colored strings attached which could be inserted into holes which gave a graphic presentation of the compass course and distance for each leg of the voyage during a particular watch. This 15th century traverse board is shown in Figure 5.

From this graphic presentation provided by the watch on duty, the pilot could then plot the ship's position on a chart. The Portuguese divided the 24 hour day into two watches beginning and ending at 0800 in the morning, but there is every indication that the Spanish and other European countries adhered to the 4 hour watch beginning and ending at 0600 in the morning. This watch timing is still in use today with the addition of two 6 hour watches during daylight hours to rotate the early morning (graveyard) shift between watches.

After Columbus decided to leave the confines of the Mediterranean (following his shipwreck in Portugal in 1476) he was to make many voyages into the known islands and lands of the Atlantic Ocean, then known as the Ocean Sea. These voyages were made both as a master or crew member on Portuguese vessels and as a chartered master and pilot on commercial trading ventures for Genoese ship owners. Most historians assert (with no foundation) that Columbus learned much of his seafaring skills and navigation from these voyages with the Portuguese, but this just doesn't stand the test of history. It was more likely the other way around.

Our history books are filled with admiration of the Portuguese sailors as leaders in the science of navigation in the 15th century, but contemporary 15th century historians didn't share that view. Peter Martyr, a renowned historian and contemporary of Columbus had this to say: "The captains of Portugal's ships were very haughty, nor did they consider that anyone better than them could know or speak of the art of navigation. And this only because of remaining in sight of land and never moving away from it, and putting into harbor every evening, they followed all that shore of Africa which on the ocean looks toward the south."

It might be said that Peter Martyr as a Spanish historian could be biased in this view, but the Portuguese historian Joao de Barros declared that: "The *Italians* were the true, first masters of the Portuguese in the nautical art; for the latter's nautical knowledge, even in the 15th century, did not allow them to lose sight of the shore."

Late in the 13th century when Ptolemais, the last remnant of the Christian East, was lost to the Islamic expansion, it was the Genoese who sailed into the Atlantic in an attempt to find a replacement sea passage to the East and so discovered the Canary Islands. Details of these early voyages (including the Phoenicians) are shrouded in myth and mystery but the later Genoese voyages of the 14th and 15th century are well documented by contemporary historians.

Both Petrarch and Boccaccio, two of the greatest European historians in the 14th century, reported expeditions of the Genoese and Florentines to the archipelago of the Canaries, then known as the "Fortunate Isles". It was a private commercial venture, led by the Genoese navigator Lanzarotto Marocello some time prior to 1338, that gave the name Lanzarote to one of the largest islands in the Canaries.

The superior and acknowledged expertise of Genoese navigators was so well established by the 15th century that many of their later voyages were performed under the sponsorship of Prince Henry the Navigator.

The Portuguese Infante, Prince Henry the Navigator founded his academy at Sagres in the 15th century to teach the shore coasting Portuguese sailors the rudiments of ocean navigation. And where did he get his teachers for the academy? From the Mediterranean, where the Moors, Venetians, and Genoese were the acknowledged leaders in ocean seamanship and navigation. For his expert Genoese navigators Prince Henry needed to go no farther than the large Genoese colony in Lisbon.

In the previous century (1317) the Portuguese monarch King Denis had founded the Portuguese Navy. Having no skilled Portuguese navigators, King Denis commissioned the Genoese Manuele Pessagno as Grand Admiral of the Navy for life (with right of hereditary succession) and instructed him to insure that the Portuguese Navy would always have 22 skilled Genoese sea-captains available to lead the fleet. It was to this Genoese colony containing skilled navigators (and cartographers) that Columbus made his way after his shipwreck in circa 1476 and from whose association he was able to maintain and improve his skill as a navigator.

It was Venetian and Genoese captains (Alvise Cadamosto and Antonio da Noli) sailing for Prince Henry who discovered and first settled the Cape Verde Islands in 1456 and 1459, the farthest any European had sailed at that time. Given these known conditions of the superiority of Genoese navigators, it is difficult for me to see why any historian would say this trained and experienced Genoese navigator named Columbus learned his skills from the Portuguese.

This dependence of the European seafaring countries on Genoese navigators went far beyond Spain's acceptance and then later dependence on the Genoese navigator Columbus for their great venture (why not depend on a Spanish or Portuguese navigator?).

So it was with England's Henry VII, when approached by another Genoese navigator in 1496 only four years after Columbus' epic voyage. This Genoese navigator proposed to cut England in on a piece of the action by discovering a route to the Indies far north of the Columbus route. Henry VII in turning down Columbus' brother and agent Bartholomew earlier, had missed the chance to be first, so he was not going to miss out this time. He commissioned this Genoese, Giovanni Coboto to sail for England on a voyage of discovery that was to lay the ground work for England's claim to the 13 American colonies.

Giovanni Coboto was none other than John Cabot, the first discoverer of North America since the Norsemen's voyages almost five centuries earlier. With a good English name like John Cabot we would think of him as a sturdy English seaman of the same stock that was to eventually rule the seas, but he was an Italian, born and raised in Genoa and learned his seafaring skills in Genoa and Venice.

France too wanted to get in on this discovery business, but since their knowledge of seafaring and navigation consisted of only fighting sea battles within sight of land, started casting around for someone to carry the French standard across the sea. Francois-Premier who succeeded Luis XII managed to commission Giovanni da Verazzano, an experienced navigator from Florence Italy who had acquired his seafaring and navigational skills in Genoa and Venice. With the reputation of Genoese navigators in general firmly established throughout Europe in the 15th century, let's return to Columbus and see if his experience would enable him to live up to this reputation.

The extent of Columbus' early Mediterranean voyages prior to 1476 and the Atlantic voyages between the years 1476 and 1485 can best be shown in a schematic chart and are graphically depicted in Figure 6. The chart shows only the voyages that can be verified from extant letters or documents. Columbus was a prolific letter writer and since so few of his letters have survived, it is reasonable to assume that these represent only a few of his many voyages. In speaking of his own wide experience at sea, he had this comment in the log on 21 December, 1492: "I have been at sea 23 years without leaving it for any time worth telling, and I have seen all the East and West, and I have travelled to Guinea, ..." Once again, with all this a matter of record how is it that some of our leading historians picture Columbus as an inexperienced and incompetent navigator who succeeded only by sheer luck?

The chart in Figure 6 also graphically illustrates why Columbus after his erudite observations and experiences at the far north and the far south and the far west of the then known Ocean Sea developed that "sea sense" and that confidence which enabled him to successfully complete his mission.

It was on these long Atlantic voyages that Columbus became a master at long distance ocean dead reckoning navigation and was to use it later with such precision as this study will show. Accurate ocean dead reckoning navigation requires: (1) the vessel be steered on a given heading with precision, (2) gauge or estimate the speed with precision, and (3) have a method of telling time so an accurate computation can be made on the distance traveled on any particular heading.

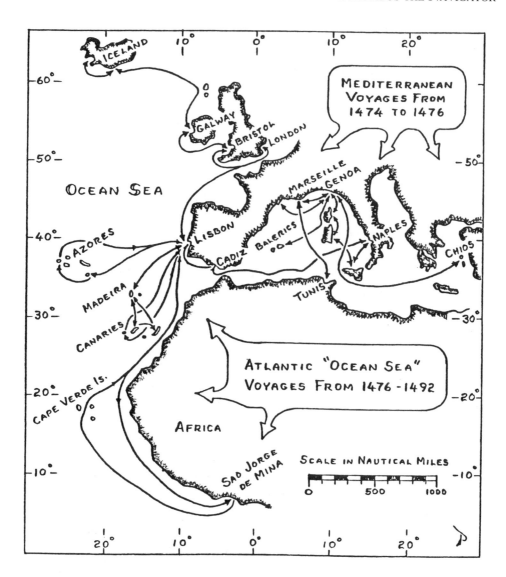

Figure 6. The recorded Mediterranean and Atlantic voyages of Columbus from 1474 to 1492.

There are those who doubt that Columbus could have obtained even a small degree of accuracy for his dead reckoning because of the crude instruments he had at his disposal. The instruments Columbus had at his disposal were indeed crude by our advanced technological standards, but let's examine each of these crude instruments and see if it would be possible for Columbus to produce an accurate dead reckoning course and log.

The magnetic compass which Columbus used for steering contained 32 points, while our modern compass is graduated in 360 degrees. This means there are 11.25 degrees between each point of the 32 point compass. This relatively large blank space between points, without the finer increment markings seen on our modern compass, leads some scholars to believe that Columbus would be incapable of adjusting to this deficiency and so his navigation is always off by 5 or 6 degrees.

And then to further compound this flawed reasoning, these same scholars state that on a long voyage these 5 to 6 degree errors would be cumulative, making termination of the steered or plotted track outrageously off. Quite the opposite is true as any statistical analyst can show. The longer the voyage and the more chances for a random error to occur, the less likely it will occur on only one side of a steered heading. In the 34 day (791 hours) discovery voyage, there would have been 198 four hour watches and with the usual changes or relief of the helmsman, would mean well over 1000 changes of helm which by laws governing random probability would narrow that postulated 5 or 6 degree error (if indeed this error ever occurred) down to an infinitesimal or negligible figure.

Further, it is inconceivable that Columbus (as well as other early pilots) having to live with the 32 point compass, would not have developed operational techniques to overcome this readily apparent deficiency of the 32 point compass. For his dead reckoning plot, Columbus was not interested in what the helmsman was steering, but what the boat was making through the water (and hopefully the same thing over the bottom). Then, since his navigation plot was relegated to one of those 32 points, he would have instructed the helmsman to favor the helm to one side or the other of a given point (in that blank 11.25 degree space) but for the purpose of his navigation would have entered in the log the exact point made good. This study will show later in the analysis of the tracks that Columbus' report of his heading for each leg was extremely accurate, indicating that for Columbus this was no crude compass with built in errors of 5 or 6 degrees.

Columbus' method of keeping time was also crude by our standards. Time was kept by the "ampolleta", a 30 minute sand glass (see Figure 5), turned and recorded by one of the ship's boys. The ship's boys were 13 and 14 year old apprentice seamen. These young apprentice seamen accounted for 60 percent of Columbus' crew. The glass time was checked and adjusted daily at the noon meridian which was obtained when the shadow of a vertical post in the center of the compass fell on the north index.

This method of keeping time could easily produce an error of 5 to 10 minutes in any one 24 hour period. While this degree of error would be disastrous in timing a 100 yard dash, when used in computing the distance covered by a slow moving sailing vessel in a 24 hour run composed of 1440

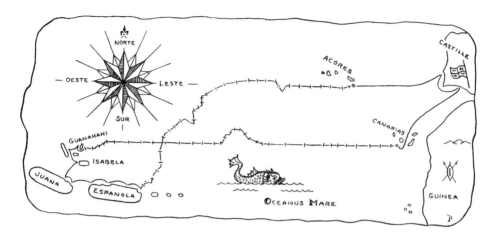

Figure 7. A postulated drawing of Columbus' portolan chart to give some indication of how he would have plotted his dead reckoning course.

minutes, the error is negligible.

Columbus as well as other pilots of his time estimated his speed by observing the bubbles or weed flowing past. Invariably a critical point is made by some scholar in this subject that an experienced yachtsman cannot estimate his speed within 1/2 knot. To draw a conclusion from that point constitutes a classic non-sequitur, ie; "since an experienced yachtsman cannot estimate his speed within 1/2 knot, it follows that Columbus could not estimate his speed within 1/2 knot." This is equating the performance of a yachtsman brought up on electronic knotmeters and has only estimated his speed a few dozen times, to the performance of a seaman, who without benefit of a modern knotmeter, has spent a lifetime estimating his speed.

This is not to say that Columbus would estimate his speed with micrometer precision on every leg, but here again his small random errors on a long voyage of many legs (His return voyage had 84 legs) would tend to average the positive and negative effect down to a negligible figure. These plotted legs of the voyage are shown in a postulated drawing of Columbus' dead reckoning chart in Figure 7.

Columbus was extremely accurate in his estimate of speed as will be shown later in this study. Yet there is an almost universal opinion among Columbian scholars that Columbus overestimated his speed to a considerable degree. This faulty opinion is brought about primarily by applying the wrong nautical mile to the league standard or factor used by Columbus and will be explained later in the analysis of my reconstructed voyages.

I have shown so far in this chapter that Columbus had the training, experience, total expertise, and tools necessary to be a capable dead reckoning navigator. Just how capable and how accurate his dead reckoning navigation proved to be will be shown and documented in Chapters 4, 5, & 6 following.

There are those who propose that Columbus used celestial navigation to calculate and maintain his desired latitude in his discovery voyage of 1492. This just doesn't stand up under severe scrutiny of his demonstrated celestial navigation expertise.

In the eight years Columbus spent in Spain awaiting action from the court, he must have realized that now was the time to read up on cosmology and astrology (the 15th century forerunner of astronomy) to use in his coming voyage and to impress the learned men of the Talavera commission. And he apparently did just that. He obtained a smattering of book knowledge of celestial navigation which he flaunted when needed, but in the actual application of which he was totally incompetent on this first 1492 voyage.

It was probably during this period in Spain when Columbus had access to and could have acquired the works of Marinus of Tyre, Ptolemy, Pierre d'Ailly, and others that he studied and annotated these works. This important point will be more fully discussed in Chapter 3 following.

He had a mariner's astrolabe and a quadrant on board for the discovery voyage in 1492 but there is absolutely no indication that he used them successfully at sea. Later while at anchor or ashore, his attempts at using a quadrant served only to illustrate his incompetence in their use which his pride would not let him admit. Just the fact that Columbus had a quadrant and astrolabe aboard his vessel has prompted many scholars to reach the conclusion that he was a master of celestial navigation, but this is an unfounded conclusion based upon a false premise.

During the Columbian era ships under government control (ie: warfare, exploration, and commercial ventures) were outfitted and supplied with stores and equipment by licensed contractors who were paid by the crown. The quadrant and astrolabe put aboard Columbus' vessels were furnished by one such contractor and were placed aboard every vessel regardless of whether the incumbent pilot or master was capable of using the instruments. When Sebastion Cabot became Spain's "Piloto Mayor" he attempted to obtain a monopoly on this lucrative trade of furnishing these instruments to the crown which was challenged in court.

The first report in the log of Columbus taking a latitude sight on Polaris with a quadrant is on 2 November, 1492, while on the northeastern shore of Cuba. He obtained a reading of 42 degrees from the equinoctial, which is about 1140 nautical miles too far north, but he dutifully entered it in the log. Morison thinks he mistook Alfirk for the north star but I find that hard to believe and feel he probably read the tangent scale instead of the 90 degree elevation (latitude) scale. This is quite possible because the Mariner's quadrant was adapted from an engineer's and surveyor's quadrant which contained several trigonometric scales in addition to the 0-90 degree elevation angle scale.

On 21 November when just a short distance down the coast, he took a second sight and again came up with the erroneous 42 degrees north latitude. This time he realized something was wrong and declared that the quadrant was broken and he would have to get it fixed when he returned to Spain. How can a quadrant be broken when the only moving part is a small weight hung on a string actuated by gravity. He simply didn't want to admit that he didn't know how to use the quadrant which had been placed aboard his vessel so it must be broken.

Columbus wasn't going to give up so on 13 December when in Moustique Bay, Haiti, he tried once more and came up with 34 degrees latitude. Once again, he was probably reading (or misreading) the tangent scale which lines up very closely with the 18 degree latitude scale which he should have been reading.

All this is rather positive proof that Columbus was unfamiliar with the practical application of celestial navigation at the time of his first voyage and so was completely dependent on his dead reckoning at which he was a master. And let me stress here that I am speaking of the first voyage only, because there is evidence to show that Columbus at a later time was to become somewhat more proficient in use of the quadrant.

In his second and third voyage he used the quadrant on five different occasions with results that varied from reasonable to bad to ridiculous. On his third crossing, Columbus found that his quadrant readings of Polaris varied by as much as 10 degrees while on the same latitude. It was these inaccurate readings that led him to believe he had been sailing uphill and nearer to the pole star thus resulting in his preposterous theory that the earth was pear shaped. Is this the same Columbus that some scholars maintain used celestial navigation with unerring accuracy because dead reckoning is so inaccurate? Really now!

However, Columbus did use the quadrant to fairly accurately establish the latitude of Jamaica (within 1/2 degree or 30 miles) on his fourth voyage. This more accurate reading was the result of averaging many observations made over a period of nearly a year from the stable platform of the grounded ships in Jamaica. These conditions certainly didn't exist on the 1492 voyage.

I can well understand the problem Columbus and the other early sailors had with use of the quadrant at sea to determine latitude. On my 1987

Figure 8. The author using a replica of a 15th century quadrant at sea.

reconstruction voyage across the Atlantic I made a replica of a 15th century quadrant with full expectation that I was going to show Columbus a thing or two about how to use it. (see Figure 8) I waited for what I considered ideal conditions, a smooth sea (with only a slight role) and a dark night where Polaris would be easy to find and line up in the sights. After eight tries I gave up! My latitudes were anywhere from 60 to 90 miles off. I first attributed this to the roll of the ship, but later I was unable to do all that much better in a quiet anchorage.

I'm not the only one who has little faith in the accuracy of a quadrant. John Davis wrote the "Seaman's Secrets", a manual for the English navy in 1587 in which he states: "The minimum equipment necessary for a skilled seaman consists of the compass, cross-staff, and chart, as the astrolabe and quadrant have proved to be very uncertain for sea observations."

Before you think that I have been too harsh in my critical remarks about Columbus' attempts at celestial observations let me assure you that he was not alone in this as all the captains and pilots (navigators) of this era were equally unschooled and depended on dead reckoning for their navigation. Listen to what Samuel Eliot Morison in his comprehensive study of early navigation has to say: "Celestial navigation formed no part of the professional pilot's or master's training in Columbus' day or for long after his death. It was practiced only by men of learning such as mathematicians, astrologers, physicians, or by gentlemen of education."

In a 5 September, 1493, royal letter of instruction for the 2nd voyage, the sovereigns advised Columbus to take along a competent "astrologo" (astronomer) to determine his latitude and longitude. This letter doesn't come right out and say so, but it quite strongly infers that the sovereigns (with their learned advisors) recognized that Columbus was unable to confirm his dead reckoning positions with accurate celestial observations (celestial navigation). Columbus did not follow the sovereigns advice as no "astrologo" was taken on the voyage. Columbus no doubt had complete faith in his dead reckoning and did not want a rival navigator aboard.

Columbus in later years was to dabble in relatively simple celestial sightings of planet conjunctions and eclipses and make irrelevant observations (mostly about the effect of conjunctions on the weather) which had no application whatsoever to his dead reckoning navigation, nor did it indicate he was using celestial navigation. Yet some naive historians down through the years have embellished these meaningless observations into a conjectural fantasy that Columbus was a learned and practicing celestial navigator far ahead of his time and the state of the art.

Columbus himself is perhaps largely responsible for promoting this fallacy by his charismatic braggadocio in his letters to the Spanish court and his influential supporters outside the court. He of course found this was necessary to uphold his exalted title of Admiral of the Ocean Sea, which was constantly under attack from rival and jealous Spanish seamen and navigators. All of this is interesting enough from a historical standpoint but has only muddied the water in recognition of Columbus' superb dead reckoning navigation which he continued to use with accuracy on all four voyages.

I have asserted that Columbus used only dead reckoning on his voyages and his navigation was accurate. Just how accurate was this dead reckoning of Columbus and other equally proficient navigators in the 15th and early 16th century? I will show in Chapters 5 & 6 that Columbus' dead reckoning from his log was within an accuracy tolerance of 0.01 percentile. But is Columbus alone among his contemporaries in performing accurate dead reckoning navigation? Not really.

Listen to what the 16th century historian Andres Bernaldez in his *Historia de los Reyes Catolicos* has to say about the accuracy of the dead reckoning navigation of experienced pilots in the Columbus era: "No one considers himself a good pilot and master who, although he has to pass from one land to another very distant without sighting any other land, makes an error of ten leagues, even in a crossing of 1000 leagues, unless the force of the tempest drives and deprives him of the use of his skill." This 10 league error within 1000 leagues agrees with my findings (Chapters 5 & 6 following) that Columbus' dead reckoning was accurate to within 0.01 percentile.

Who is this Andre Bernaldez and does he have the credentials to make such an authoritative statement about the accuracy of 16th century navigation? Bernaldez in writing his *Historia* was a contemporary and confidant of Columbus and other leading members of the court involved in the enterprise, and so would have been privy to official records of the era. The records of this extensive Atlantic shipping (called "Carrera de Indias") are still available in the "Archivo General de Indias" in Seville.

Bernaldez would have known that beginning with the re-supply voyage of Bartolome Colon (Columbus' brother) in 1494 and extending through the year 1549, there were 396 recorded voyages that left Spain and successfully arrived at their initial destination on Hispaniola using these so-called "crude" 16th century dead reckoning methods and instruments. So the stated opinion of Bernaldez, borne out by these undisputed historical facts, certainly establishes the fact that late 15th and early 16th century dead reckoning navigation was both accurate and in general use.

I have shown how Columbus developed the navigational expertise to accurately navigate his vessels across the Atlantic to his destination. And in the previous Chapter I showed his overwhelming drive to discover the westward route to the Indies. Now let's examine how he accomplished this epic feat in his "Enterprise of the Indies".

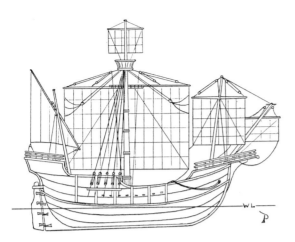

3

The "Enterprise of the Indies"

When the Spanish sovereigns finally approved Columbus' plan to discover the westward route to the Indies in 1492, he promptly named it the "Enterprise of the Indies." Columbus had first proposed his (then unnamed) plan to King John II of Portugal in 1483 by which time it had to be a well organized and documented plan for the court to even consider it. Just when and how was this momentous plan conceived? Columbus himself probably couldn't give us a finite date as the plan probably slowly emerged in his mind sometime during his Atlantic voyages.

Columbus was a genius and a visionary whose mind could penetrate far above the mundane obstacles that shackled the minds and actions of his fellow seamen. He needed no tall tales from other pilots, or obscure passages in ancient documents to inspire him. The vision of his plan came by intuition from within his own fertile mind. Most historians refuse to believe this and search endlessly for some substantive or logical reason for Columbus' inspired plan.

Some historians insist that the plan was a result of hearing the Norse tales of lands to the west during his voyage to Iceland in 1476. At first glance this seems reasonable enough but it flies in the face of known facts. Both Ferdinand in his biography and Las Casas in his history affirm that Columbus only began to consider projects of discovery after his marriage to Felipa Perestrello in 1479 and his stay on Porto Santo in 1480-1482. A key factor here would be the charts of the Ocean Sea (Atlantic) that Columbus inherited from his wife's seafaring father. Further it is quite clear from Columbus' writings (and indeed his four voyages) that he believed any land worth discovering lay well to the south of even the Azores and the Canaries, much less Iceland.

To further pin down the date after 1479, it is quite clear that Columbus' plan was well under way when he corresponded with Toscanelli during 1481. Paolo del Pozzo Toscanelli was a learned Florentine mathematician and cosmographer who corresponded with both the Portuguese court and Columbus concerning the feasibility of sailing west across the Ocean Sea to reach the Indies. Here I must pause and address the fact that some historians (foremost of whom is Vignaud) claim that the Toscanelli correspondence never occurred and was fraudulently concocted by Columbus. The overwhelming evidence in this case would support the contemporary 16th century reports of both Ferdinand and Las Casas that the correspondence was genuine, rather than the conclusions of 19th and 20th century scholars who base their opinions that they are false on strained and tortured analysis of the Latin rhetoric used in the extant documents (which may be poor copies) in the archives of Spain.

The Toscanelli correspondence to both the Portuguese court (Canon Fernao Martíns) and to Columbus contains reference to a chart which presumably accompanied the letters. This chart has never been found and historians have long debated just what was on the chart. The chart is significant as it was a factor in the preparation of his plan and his later navigation of the route. Columbus mentions the chart in his letters, and in his log infers it is the chart he sent to Martín Alonzo Pinzón on the Pinta mid-way on the voyage. He then later retrieved it and conferred with Pinzón on what the chart indicated.

Most reconstructions of the chart are based on Martin Behaim's world globe because Behaim is thought to have used Toscanelli's projections in preparation of his globe. That hardly stands up to the fact that the globe's explanatory tables give a complete list of the sources which includes both the ancient cosmographers (Ptolemy, Strabo, Pomponius Mela, Pliny, etc.) and contemporary sources, and Toscanelli is not among them. A Mercator projection of the North Atlantic portion of Behaim's globe is shown in Figure 22, Chapter 6, following.

Toscanelli's description of the chart is very ambiguous but suggests that it was a simplified ungraduated (lacking latitude and longitude segments) rectangular projection, not intended for navigation but just to show the linear and azimuth positions of Cathay, Cipangu, the Indies, and the intervening undiscovered islands in relation to the Azores, Canaries, and the shores of western Europe. Without pretending it to be a studied or accurate reconstruction, I have shown in Figure 9, a postulated example of what Toscanelli's chart would have resembled.

The dates of the Toscanelli correspondence together with dates of the

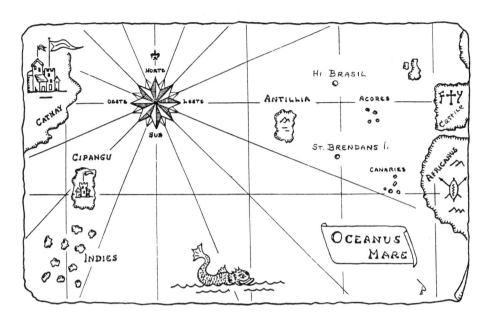

Figure 9. A postulated chart of the "Ocean Sea" such as Paolo Toscanelli would have furnished to Columbus.

preceding activity would then establish the date of conceiving the plan in the period between late 1479 and early 1481.

Now that the date is out of the way we must ask what inspired and motivated Columbus to formulate his plan to "buscar el levante por el Poniente." seek the East by going west.

Over a period of time there have appeared concocted stories of an ancient chart that Columbus somehow found and kept secret, or a dying pilot who had been blown across the Atlantic to the New World and then fought his way back to gasp out the secret just before he died in Columbus' arms. Even the 16th century Spanish historians Las Casas and Oviedo repeated similar apocryphal stories possibly with a view to demeaning Columbus in order to reserve the glory of the discovery for Spain. All of these have been shown to be transparent fictional nonsense and probably derive from a belief that before Columbus would risk his life, he would require positive proof of his destination, rather than just an opinion based on unproven facts.

Most historians believe that it was Columbus' reading and study of the ancient geographers and philosophers such as Marinus of Tyre, Strabo, Ptolemy, Pierre d'Ailly, Aristotle, and Senaca that inspired his plan. Indeed his son Ferdinand infers this in his biography, and Columbus' annotated notes in some of these works also seems to confirm this theory.

The problem with this theory is that Columbus did not date his annotations so we don't know when he made them. Then a study of when these key documents would have been available to Columbus indicates that either they had not yet been published or that he would not have access to them until he went to Spain in 1485.

The Tractatus de Imagine Mundi (Imago Mundi) by Cardinal Pierre d'Ailly is the document containing the most annotated notes by Columbus. This is also the volume which contains the most information to support Columbus' plan. The first copies of this work were published in Louvain between 1480 and 1483. This was the period when Columbus was in Porto Santo and Madeira and had already conceived his plan and there is no way he could have even heard of the document much less have one in his possession. So it is obvious these annotated references were made long after his plan was conceived and were intended solely to support and prove his plan to the skeptical court of Spain.

There have been other theories for Columbus' inspiration or "secret" put forward, such as Columbus stealing an early copy of Toscanelli's chart from the Portuguese (proposed by Madariaga), and then an equally preposterous "predescubrimiento" or secret voyage in which he had previously discovered the islands (proposed by Luis Ulloa) which made him so sure of his task and which convinced the Franciscans of La Rábida to support him. These theories fall in the realm of fantasy and are so obviously transparent nonsense that I refuse to do any more than just report them to the reader.

One fact that is paramount to development of the plan in Columbus' mind was his conviction that; "il mondo e poco," the world is small. To be more specific, Columbus believed that a degree of longitude at the equator was only 56 2/3rd Arabic miles. Then by some convoluted interpretation of the writings of early Arab and Greek cosmographers (Alfragan, Eratosthenes, Ptolemy) he arrived at the conclusion that the length of the Arabic degree was 45 nautical miles at the equator and 40 nautical miles at the latitude of the Canaries from which he would be sailing.

His rationale in this instance was primarily based on the writings of Marinus of Tyre who advocated a much smaller circumference of the earth, and on Toscanelli who advocated a much smaller breath of the Ocean Sea (using Ptolemy's circumference of the earth), rather than the larger figures of either Eratosthenes or Alfragan who were more nearly correct. Columbus also believed there was only 60 degrees of longitude between the Canaries and Cipangu (Japan) so that would make his proposed voyage to the Indies only 2400 nautical miles (60 X 40) long.

It is apparent that this ingrained conviction preceded his attempts to prove or substantiate this "small world" to the Spanish court by quoting the ancient geographers and philosophers referenced above. Where then did this conviction or insight originate?

The Swiss historian, Jacob Burckhardt, one of the greatest of the 19th century historians, put forward the theory that all early Genoese and other Mediterranean navigators were taught and firmly believed in the "small world" concept. Burckhardt writes: "The crusades had opened unknown distances to the European mind, and awakened in all the passion for travel and adventure. It may be hard to indicate precisely the point where this passion allied itself with, or became servant of, the thirst for knowledge; but it was in Italy that this was first and most completely the case." He then goes on to show that it was this "small world" concept together with this ingrained thirst for knowledge that spurred the Genoese and Venetian sailors to become the leaders in ocean navigation and fearlessly pursue their voyages into the Atlantic in the 13th, 14th, and 15th century to discover the Canaries and the Cape Verde Islands.

Columbus had thus inherited from his Genoese navigator forbears the inborn faith that the world was not so impossibly large and forbidding that it could not be conquered! Then this faith together with the Genoese trait of an insatiable thirst for knowledge led inevitably to his plan.

But the real "secret" for the successful completion of that grandiose plan lies in Columbus' character, his genius, his exceptional global sense of the sea, and a conviction that he was the one ordained by destiny to perform the task.

Once the plan was approved, Columbus lost no time in hurrying to Palos to get his "Enterprise of the Indies" underway. Why Palos?

The immediate reason for centering the "Enterprise of the Indies" in Palos was that the port city was assessed by the crown to furnish two vessels for the enterprise because of some unstated past violations. For Columbus this was fortunate indeed because Palos had proved crucial to Columbus' earlier reception in Spain and was now to emerge as a vital and decisive force in the enterprise by providing the necessary seaworthy ships and then the able and competent officers and men to man the ships.

The city was also where two of Columbus' most faithful supporters resided. The first and most important was Fray Antonio de Marchena, head of the Franciscan monastery La Rábida at Palos, who befriended Columbus in 1485 when he had just journeyed (fled would be a better word) from Portugal to Spain. Columbus was fortunate that his first encounter in Spain was in a monastery of the Franciscan order.

The Franciscan order took more interest in discovery of new lands to spread the faith than any other branch of the church. It was Franciscan monks

Figure 10. Columbus with his young son Diego approaching the monastery of "La Rábida" on his arrival in Spain.

who preceded Marco Polo into the Far East and China and established missions which flourished in the late 13th and early 14th century. The Franciscan Giovanni da Montecorvino was archbishop of the diocese of Peking from 1289 to around 1306 and he was followed by Franciscans who visited Malabar, Calicut, Canganor, Sumatra, Java, Canton, Zayton, and Nanking. But all of this came to an end with the conquests of Tamerlane and the expansion of Islam in the late 14th and early 15th century when the land route to the Far East was cut off.

Marchena would have been familiar with this history of the Franciscan missions to the Far East so it follows that he would be vitally interested in a project that would help the Franciscans and the church regain its toe hold in that area of the world. Marchena was both a man of God and a learned cosmographer, so he could easily see that Columbus had the answer and was just the man to be "God's navigator" to carry Christianity back to the Far East (the Indies) by a sea route to bypass the blockade of Islam.

It was for this reason that Fray Marchena steadfastly supported Columbus from that first meeting in La Rábida through his lengthy petition before the court. Marchena was respected and admired by both Ferdinand and Isabela so he was the most dominant force in the final approval of Columbus' plan.

With his plan finally approved by the court, Columbus was now to receive even more support when Marchena assisted him in gathering together his officers and crew from the Palos, Moguer, and Huelva area.

Columbus' other supporter from the Palos area was Juan de La Cosa, a ship owner who had promised Columbus a ship for the enterprise some years earlier when Columbus was fighting his way through the court. Historians are in disagreement as to whether this is the same Juan de La Cosa who was to later draw his now famous map of the New World, however for the purpose of this study the question is moot. La Cosa at this time furnished Columbus a large vessel which Columbus named the "Santa Maria" and commissioned it his flagship.

The "Santa Maria", the largest of the three and so naturally the flagship, was a nao or cargo ship, bulky and broad beamed, probably around 80 feet in length and capable of carrying about 100 tons of cargo. His flagship was originally named "La Gallega", the woman of Galacia and later named "Marigalante", Naughty Mary. Columbus of course frowned on both of these names and re-named her "Santa Maria", Holy Mary.

The "Pinta" was a square rigged caravel smaller and lighter (probably about 70 feet in length) and built for speed rather than cargo capacity. This was one of the vessels no doubt reluctantly contributed to Columbus by the city of Palos. The name "La Pinta" (painted woman) was a sailor's euphemism

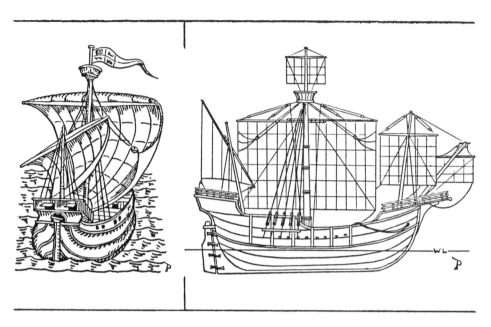

Figure 11. The "Santa Maria" as depicted in a 15th century wood cut, and the plan of the Spanish replica built in Barcelona for the 1992 Quincentennial Celebration. Of the two rigs shown, the 16th century woodcut is the most authentic as the trapezoidal topsail on the Barcelona replica did not appear until late in the 16th century.

for a prostitute and although Columbus probably didn't like that name either, he wisely let it stand in deference to the Spanish sailors who saw nothing wrong with it.

The "Niña" was a lateen rigged caravel, the smallest but possibly the fastest of the vessels contributed by Palos and was probably about 65 feet in length. The name "La Niña" meant simply The Girl and this vessel was Columbus' favorite in which he returned to Spain after losing the Santa Maria and was to use her again in his later voyages. The tall triangular lateen rig was not well adapted to downwind work so Columbus changed the Niña to a square rig in the Canaries prior to setting out on his discovery voyage. This change of rig is shown in Figure 12.

When Columbus arrived in Palos on 23 May, 1492, he had his three ships but no officers or crew. Although the crown had promised four months advance pay, not a single sailor came forward to sign on for the voyage. The sailors of Palos were not lacking in courage or experience in ocean voyages so why this reluctance? The real reason for this reluctance was twofold.

First, the sailors had a natural native distrust for this foreigner who for all they knew couldn't even row a boat much less command ocean going

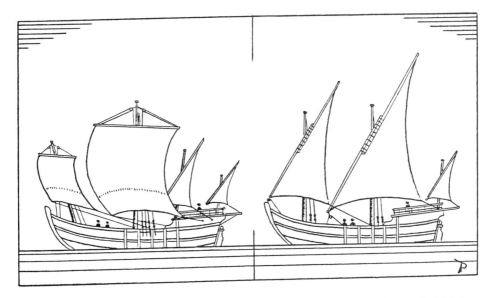

Figure 12. The caravel "Niña" before and after the sail change from a lateen rig (right) to a square rig.

vessels. Secondly, and perhaps most important was the sailor's understandable fear of sailing into unknown seas with only the promise of this strange foreigner that there was land out there that they would discover then return safely home. The crown had set a deadline in which Columbus must get his enterprise underway so it now appeared that after all these years of fighting for his cause, he would fail for lack of a crew to man the ships.

As 2 June, the deadline set by the crown approached, Columbus appealed for help to his friend and mentor Fray Marchena at nearby La Rábida monastery. Marchena then introduced Columbus to Martín Alonzo Pinzón in what can only be described as a momentous fateful occasion.

Martín Alonzo Pinzón was from a wealthy ship owning family in Palos and was respected and admired by the seamen of the area, many of whom had sailed with him on his extensive ocean voyages. After listening to Columbus explain his plan, Martín Alonzo was able to recognize that this Genoese seaman was an extraordinarily competent navigator who had a viable enterprise which he should join.

From there on it was easy. Martín Alonzo assumed captaincy of the Pinta and brought along his brother Vicente Yañez (an equally experienced captain) to be captain of the Niña. The seamen of the Palos, Moguer, and Huelva area now flocked to join the enterprise because of their unquestioned faith in the Pinzón brothers.

Historians are divided in their opinion of the role that Pinzón played in the overall success of the voyage. Understandably the Spaniards tend to exaggerate it while the Italians tend to underestimate it. The answer is probably somewhere between the two views. However there can be no doubt about what the inhabitants of Palos think, as a large heroic statue of Pinzón in the mid-town Plaza is emblazoned with this pronouncement: "The Discoverer of America - Martín Alonzo Pinzón."

From this point on, Columbus' 1492 voyage resulting in the discovery of the New World has had more books and papers written about it than any other event in history with the possible exception of the birth of Christ. The historic event of Columbus' landfall and landing on a small island in the Bahamas which the Indians called Guanahani has been celebrated and venerated in textbooks, novels, poetry, and art down through the centuries. But as the exciting story of the subsequent conquest and colonization of the New World unfolded, the actual location of this small but historically important island was lost or misplaced by historians and cartographers. In the late 18th century a search was begun by historical scholars to find Columbus' lost landfall island of Guanahani which continues to this day.

This search for Guanahani has a long history, shrouded in mystery by lost historical documents and charts. The Bahamas, then called the Lucayan (Lucayos) islands were largely forgotten by history in the 16th and 17th century because the discoverers and colonizers from western Europe quickly moved on to more profitable and exciting lands. The docile and friendly Taino Indians who met Columbus were soon hauled away to Spain or Hispaniola as slaves early in the 16th century and for nearly two centuries the islands lay largely unpopulated except by freebooters and pirates. So it is no wonder there was a general "who cares" attitude toward the question of which of these islands was the Columbus landfall.

Finally the problem was addressed when the Spanish historian, Juan Buatista Muñoz, having been commissioned by Spain's king Charles III, in the years between 1779-1793, wrote a comprehensive and thoroughly researched history of the New World, naming Watling Island (the present San Salvador) as the Columbus landfall. He doesn't give any geographical or navigational reason for this, (which is apparently why some scholars disregard his finding) but we do know that he had made an intensive search and study of Spanish archives which at the time probably contained many historical documents and charts that have since been dispersed or lost. With this in mind, it is hard to believe that we should not give his identification of Watling Island (San Salvador) as the landfall some legitimacy as historical truth.

But the landfall question really came alive in 1825 when Martín

Fernández Navarrete discovered and published the Bartolome de Las Casas summary of Columbus' long lost original log. Much of the Las Casas summary of the log consists of verbatim quotes in Columbus' own words and the rest is abridged and summarized in the words of Las Casas. The navigational data for most of the voyage has been left largely intact and will be analyzed and discussed in Chapters 5 and 6.

The Las Casas Columbus log, written in 16th century script was subsequently translated into Italian, German, and finally English. The publication of the log provoked an intensive effort by scholars from around the world to identify Guanahani, the Columbus landfall island, from interpretation of the navigational data in the log.

Navarette, after discovering the log, was the first to do this, naming Grand Turk island, just southeast of the Caicos Islands as the landfall. This was later supported by the historian writer Samuel Kettel (Boston 1827) followed by George Gibbs (New York 1846) and currently has been quite convincingly supported by my colleague, the late Robert Power.

The Grand Turk theory held sway for a while but was soon replaced by Cat Island, further north in the Bahamas, and first proposed by the well known writer Washington Irving with his naval advisor Alexander Mackenzie. Mackenzie must have been an arm chair sailor indeed because in tracing the Columbus inter-island track he led Columbus with his 7 and 8 foot draft boats across waters between Great Exuma and Long Island that you can practically walk across and hardly get your feet wet. But nevertheless the Cat Island theory held on and was later given a boost when supported by such international heavyweight scholars of the period as Jean Barnard de la Roquette, Alexander von Humbolt, and the Baron de Montlezun.

By the middle of the 19th century Grand Turk and Cat Island were ahead in this name-the-landfall game when the British navy captain A. B. Becher published his book *The Landfall of Columbus* (London 1856). This book was a scholarly approach by an experienced navigator and seaman. It contained an analysis of the trans-Atlantic track and a large fold out accurately scaled chart of the Bahamas on which he traced the route of Columbus from Guanahani through the several islands he discovered on the way to Cuba. Becher put forward a lucid and convincing theory to again name Watling Island (following Muñoz) as the landfall site.

But Becher was primarily a seaman and navigator and was not readily accepted by the academic community (I can understand that) until supported by R. H. Majors, the well known writer of the day, who switched his view from Navarette (Grand Turk) to Becher's view. Becher was on the right track and was far ahead of his time on most points but he was soon to be overshadowed by a spate of entries into the field.

Now the search for Guanahani was warming up. The contestants were Grand Turk, Cat Island, Watling Island, and now a fourth, Mayaguana was added in 1864 by a scholarly Brazilian historian, Francisco Adolpho de Varnhagen. I find it difficult to give much weight to Varnhagen's views since he also produced a contrived and geographically impossible chart and thesis to try and prove that Amerigo Vespucci actually made his fictitious 1497 voyage. Varnhagen's theory held sway for a while but was soon to be replaced by yet another in a theory proposed by Gustavus V. Fox, a U.S.Navy captain who had served as assistant Secretary of the Navy under Abraham Lincoln.

Fox named Samana Cay as the landfall island and put forward a convincing argument and a critical analysis of the previously proposed landfall sites to prove his point. Joseph Judge, a senior editor of the *National Geographic* magazine at a much later date (1986) was to adopt this theory nearly intact.

The next serious scholar to enter the scene was J. B. Murdock who wrote an essay on the itinerary of Columbus through the Bahamas which was published in the U.S.Naval Institute *Proceedings* in April 1884. Murdock's essay contained a criticism of previous theories then returned to Watling Island (now San Salvador), the original landfall designated by Muñoz nearly a century earlier. Murdock also provided a postulated track through the islands which was later (1942) to be adopted and refined with minor changes by Samuel Eliot Morison.

This Murdock/Morison track together with Morison's strong argument on how the geographical features of San Salvador (Watling Island) fit the description of Guanahani seemed to satisfy historians and geographers alike for the next several decades. But this respite from controversy was to come to an end in 1947 when Pieter Verhoog published a book *Guanahani Again* in which he named South Caicos Island as the landfall. Pieter Verhoog was a respected professional ship's captain and navigator and his theory found a warm reception in the U.S.Naval Institute. The well known navigator, Captain P.V.H. Weems writing in the *Proceedings* of the U.S.Naval Institute, lauded Verhoog as providing the answer to the Columbus landfall question. Verhoog's theory was later given more support by the somewhat contrived research of Edwin and Marian Link.

Egg island, northwest of Eleuthera is one of the latest (and sixth) of the new islands in this list, having been proposed by Arne Molander in 1981. Molander presented a scholarly and painstakingly documented paper supporting his view to the Society for the History of Discoveries at the University of Minnesota in October 1988 where I presented one of my first research papers on my empirical reconstruction of Columbus' voyage as outlined in this book.

In all this proliferation of islands and their advocates, the strongest and most widely accepted was the theory proposed first in 1942 by the respected historian and writer Samuel Eliot Morison, naming San Salvador (formally Watling Island) as the landfall site. This landfall theory was part of Morison's Voluminous two volume book, *Admiral of the Ocean Sea* which has become the bible for students of the life of Columbus and his voyages.

Morison was supported in his research by U.S. Navy captain John W. McElroy (who plotted Columbus' track across the Atlantic) and by Senor Mauricio Obregon, the Ambassador at Large from Columbia and eminent Columbian historian. Obregon in 1989 sailed the Morison track from San Salvador to Cuba and after adding some minor revisions declared it still the best and most accurate rendition of Columbus' log. One of the best and the most authoritative support for Morison's theory of San Salvador as the landfall island is contained in the monumental biography of Columbus by Paolo Emilio Taviani; *Christopher Columbus–The Grand Design*, and in several other essays he has written on the subject. And finally the latest strong support for the Morison theory is from William F. Keegan in his acclaimed prehistory of the Bahamas: *The People Who Discovered Columbus*, published by the University Press of Florida.

Morison was so widely acclaimed and accepted that the question of where Columbus landed seemed forever settled until Joseph Judge published his article in the November 1986 issue of the prestigious *National Geographic* magazine.

Judge named the small, barren, and uninhabited Samana Cay as Guanahani, the landfall of Columbus. He supports his argument with a computer projection of the Atlantic track leading to Samana Cay, followed by a tortured and contrived reconstruction of the portion of Columbus' log which covered the track from the landfall island to Cuba. The article contains beautiful (but misleading or irrelevant) photographs and several impressive graphic presentations of a number of computer studies which are up to the usual high quality standard of the *National Geographic* magazine. However, the academic quality and the historical and geographical accuracy of the written thesis which these visual aids are supposed to support has been a disappointment to many of the long time members of the society such as myself. Analysis of the theory proposed by the National Geographic Society is contained in Chapters 6 & 7.

This brings us up to the point where I entered into the controversy. My several research voyages (1985,87,90,91) and the resulting academic papers give a true picture of the navigational expertise of Columbus and shows rather conclusively that San Salvador (Watling's Island) is the true landfall of Columbus, and provides the basis for this book.

A number of enthusiastic but naive scholars have recently appeared on the scene with poorly substantiated theories which either support previously named islands or name such unlikely (unbelievable would be a better word) candidates as Great Harbour Cay, Conception Islands, and the Plana Cays. These new landfall islands (which brings our candidates to nine) have been obtained by digging into the fertile ground of the inter-island track with its vague and romanticized descriptions of the islands along the track.

⚓ ⚓ ⚓ ⚓ ⚓ ⚓ ⚓ ⚓

During the seven years I was engaged in my Columbus voyage research I finally got caught up in the excitement generated by the 1992 Quincentennial Celebration of Columbus' discovery of the New World. This was a great one time event that I could not afford to miss, as at my age I could hardly wait another 500 years for the chance. Accordingly I organized a re-creation of Columbus' voyage to be performed by three American yachts (representing the Santa Maria, Pinta, and Niña) who would sail Columbus' route from Palos, Spain to San Salvador, Bahamas on the exact 500th anniversary of the historic voyage.

My project was appropriately named the 1492/1992 "Enterprise of the Indies" and was sanctioned an official USA Quincentenary Maritime Event by the President's Jubilee Commission in Washington. I then obtained the participation of the Quincentennial Commissions of the Bahamas, Spain, and Italy to make it an International Event by an exchange of flags to be carried on the vessels both ways (following the route of Columbus) between the Old World and the New World.

Obtaining the other two boats to join "Gooney Bird" was no small task as I had set a rather high standard for both the vessel and the skipper since we were representing the USA in an official event and I didn't want anything to go awry. This was especially important since we would be making the crossing (like Columbus) at the height of the hurricane season.

The first boat to join me was Tom Hails in his Allied 36 ketch "Princess". Tom is an experienced ocean sailor that I have known for years and his vessel (like "Gooney Bird") is designed and built for blue water passages. When he first contacted me (1990) he was sailing the "Princess" around the world (in Australia at the time) and agreed to meet me in late July, 1992, in Palos Spain for the start of the 1492/1992 "Enterprise of the Indies" re-enactment.

Tom and his First Mate (and she insists the Last) Pat Stovall are real go-getters and during early 1992 procured sticker emblems, miniature flags, and T-shirts with the "Enterprise of the Indies" logo I had designed, to be given out along the way. And Pat designed and made a costume of 15th century sailor's clothing for Tom and me that would have made Columbus and Pinzón green with envy. I was unable to find a suitable third boat so "Gooney Bird" and "Princess" were the yachts that sailed the event.

Late in 1991 and again in 1992 I sailed into the Huelva/Palos harbor and moored at the Club Maritimo de Huelva at the Old World destination of my "Enterprise of the Indies" Quincentennial Celebration Event. I might explain that it is no longer possible for a sailing vessel to get to nearby Palos because it is cut off by a low fixed bridge over the silted up and shallow Tinto river. I received what can only be called a hero's welcome by the gracious people of the area. (see Figure 13)

At this time I presented a flag of the "Enterprise of the Indies" to Pilar Bulgar, the Mayor (Alcaldesa) of Palos to represent a gift from the New World to the Old World. Pilar in turn gave me a beautiful flag of the city and an inscribed bronze plaque to commemorate my visit. This was my third meeting with Pilar as I had met her first in 1987, when I attended the Phileas Society seminar on Columbus held at La Rábida in Palos, then again in 1991 at the termination of my research of the return voyage of Columbus.

Pilar could very well be the only female mayor in male dominated Spanish politics and has recently acquired more honors in becoming a member of Parliament representing the area. She has done wonders for the city in improving living conditions and providing parks to preserve the historic heritage of the city. Indeed, Pilar is so well loved by the people that no one bothers to run against her for re-election.

Columbus Day is celebrated in the Huelva/Palos area on 3 August the date Columbus departed Palos on his epic voyage. In the preceding week which they call their "Colombinas" there are receptions, banquets, sporting events, street fairs, and yacht regattas. I was invited to a number of these and came away with so many gift plaques, medallions, and scrolls to commemorate my voyage that they have spilled over from my office to a display in the Bradenton Yacht Club.

Tom in the "Princess" was supposed to join me during this time but he had run into a problem with his boat in South Africa and didn't make it. I departed Palos in "Gooney Bird" the afternoon of 3 August exactly 500 years after Columbus and headed south for the Canaries following in his wake. Once I left the confused winds near shore, I settled "Gooney Bird" into a pleasant downwind run to the Canaries pushed along by the moderate northeast trade winds off the coast of Africa.

8/HUELVA INFORMACION
CAPITAL   DOMINGO 6 DE OCTUBRE DE 1991

Douglas Peck es un auténtico aventurero. A bordo de su embarcación. 'Gooney Bird' llegó el pasado 23 de septiembre hasta nuestra provincia (desde Florida) y tiene previsto el próximo domingo día 13 volver a cruzar el Océano Atlántico para reproducir el primer viaje que realizó el almirante Cristóbal Colón hace 499 años. Pero lo más asombroso de esta hazaña es que el norteamericano, de 73 años de edad, lo hace en solitario.

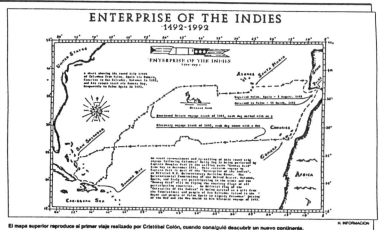

El mapa superior reproduce el primer viaje realizado por Cristóbal Colón, cuando consiguió descubrir un nuevo continente.

Siguiendo la ruta atlántica de Cristóbal Colón

Douglas Peck repetirá exactamente el primer viaje colombino 500 años después

JAVIER ÁLVAREZ DE MIRANDA

Dicen que el poder y la capacidad de superación del hombre no tiene límites, y desde luego un buen exponente de ello es Douglas Peck. Este norteamericano, de 73 años de edad, es un auténtico amante de la aventura, y trata de repetir la gesta realizada por Cristóbal Colón.

Cuando en el año 1964 este hombre nacido en Tenesee se retiró de las Fuerzas Aéreas Norteamericanas decidió cambiar una de sus pasiones: el aire, por otra: la mar. Desde entonces ha navegado realizando ya dos travesías atlánticas completas en los años 85 y 87. Ahora, su embarcación 'Gooney Bird' se encuentra amarrada en el Club Marítimo de Huelva y allí estará hasta el próximo día 13 de octubre, cuando junto a las réplicas de las tres carabelas, partirá hacia la isla canaria de La Gomera para posteriormente poner la proa de su barco rumbo a San Salvador (donde espera llegar a mediados de noviembre) y más tarde finalizar su viaje a mediados de diciembre, cuando atraque en el puerto de Florida (Estados Unidos). Lo más asombroso de todo

El aventurero norteamericano Douglas Peck, a bordo de su embarcación 'Gooney Bird'.

A bordo de su embarcación, el 'Gooney Bird', Douglas Peck tratará de repetir, el próximo año y con toda exactitud, el primer viaje colombino, 500 años después de que el almirante descubriera un nuevo mundo

prostituta. Hace falta mucho valor para adentrarse en el océano y recorrer miles de millas náuticas. También comenta Peck que está muy bien acompañado "por tres barriles de ron".

Embarcación

Su embarcación (tipo crucero) tiene 31 pies, 10 metros aproximadamente, y está construido en fibra de vidrio. Cuenta con un motor diesel de cuatro cilindros con 27 caballos de potencia. Además está equipado con los elementos más avanzados en navegación (radio decamétrica, fax meteorológico, etc). Como cualquier mortal, durante su travesía necesita dormir, pero lo hace en pequeñas siestas, de 30 minutos, hasta que completa unas seis horas al día.

"No soy una persona anti-social -declara- me gusta la gente, pero cuando estoy en la mar me encuentro verdaderamente a gusto y me olvido de todos mis problemas".

No todo en la vida de Peck es aventura, con sus travesías está realizando diversas investigaciones para varias universidades

Figure 13. A copy of a portion of one of the articles on my 1492-1992 "Enterprise of the Indies" USA Quincentenary Maritime Event that was given wide distribution in the Spanish Press.

I stayed at Las Palmas on Gran Canaria and was there for their "Colombinas" which they celebrate from 25 August to 1 September, the time Columbus was supposed to be there repairing the rudder of Pinta and provisioning the ships. Tom and Pat finally joined me there and we were feted by the governor of the island (resplendent in our 15th century costumes) at dinners and receptions where we were given gifts and plaques to commemorate our visit.

I departed Las Palmas on 2 September for what I thought would be a pleasant overnight sail to Gomera in the light to moderate northeast trade winds. It wasn't! I learned very quickly that when the moderate trade winds funnel down through the venturi between Gran Canaria and Tenerife and again between Tenerife and Gomera, the usually moderate trade winds build up to sustained gale force winds. After an unpleasant and punishing 36 hour thrash, I made it into the rather exposed harbor at San Sebastion on Gomera and anchored just before dark. The next several days were spent repairing the damage I had sustained to my jib, mainsail, and Bimini top. My fingers are still sore from the 1000 (at least) stitches I had to put in the torn seams of my mainsail.

Tom and Pat in the "Princess" joined me in Gomera about two days later as their departure from Las Palmas had been delayed by some problem with the boat. They went ashore in San Sebastion but I was reluctant to leave "Gooney Bird" because of the possibility of the anchor dragging in the gusty winds and surge of the exposed harbor. I had already been forced to re-set my anchor twice during my stay in the harbor, so at this late date I didn't want to jeopardize my whole project by having "Gooney Bird" washed up on the beach while I was ashore blissfully having a rum and coke.

According to my approved plan we were scheduled to leave Gomera in the "Enterprise of the Indies" re-enactment on 6 September exactly 500 years after Columbus. Here again Tom was unable to leave because of a problem with some new sails he had recently procured and said he would catch up with me along the way. I departed Gomera in "Gooney Bird" the morning of 6 September on the anniversary of Columbus' departure and sailed a southwesterly course to reach 24 degrees latitude then sailed due west which put me right in to San Salvador. This was pre-arranged so Tom sailing later on the same latitude could catch up and join me in the crossing. I should hasten to say that on this voyage I was not trying to exactly adhere to Columbus' track as I had on my previous research voyages.

I had an unusually fast passage across the Atlantic and arrived of San Salvador five days before the 12 October landing. My original intention if I arrived early was to hove-to and await the 12 October date and time for my arrival. But I had not anticipated such a long wait bobbing around uncomfortably in six foot seas, so I proceeded on in and anchored off the western shore of San Salvador to be there for the Quincentennial landfall celebration on Columbus Day, 12 October. Tom had not caught up with me on the way across but he made it into the anchorage in the early morning hours of 12 October to join in the celebration.

The Quincentennial Celebration on San Salvador was a disappointment to me as it consisted largely of commercialized circus-like hoopla aimed at the tourist. In the preceding two years I had made detailed plans for my participation in the celebration with the then acting commissioner Christfield Johnson to be centered around the Columbus Museum on the island. All this went down the drain when I found that Johnson had been removed from office (no one even knew where he was) and the new commissioner didn't know a thing about these arrangements or my well publicized official USA Quincentenary Maritime Event that was so well received in Spain and the Canary Islands.

At least I have the satisfaction of knowing that I sailed Columbus' route from his departure in Palos, Spain through the Canaries to his landfall on San Salvador on the 500th anniversary of his historic voyage and no one else can make that claim. And Tom can be equally satisfied with his accomplishment of sailing Columbus' route across the Atlantic from Gomera to San Salvador on this historic 500th anniversary. Granted things didn't go exactly as planned but no one can take away this feeling of personal satisfaction that we have earned for a unique accomplishment.

I have shown that the history of the search for Columbus' landfall by many scholars produced nine different answers (or islands) even though they all based their findings on the same navigational data in the Las Casas Columbus log. In the following chapters, I will show why this hodge-podge of findings exists and why my pragmatic and scientific method of using a sailing vessel to reconstruct the track will provide the right answers concerning the accuracy of Columbus' navigation and pinpoint the true landfall island.

4

Methodology Used in Reconstruction of Columbus' Voyage

The empirical research methodology of using a sailboat as a test vehicle in reconstruction of the 1492-1493 discovery voyage is new to this particular field of historical research. As I pointed out in my Introduction, the rather conservative academic community is reluctant to accept a new concept in historical research, particularly one that challenges their beloved computers.

Some of this negative reaction stems from the fact that ocean navigation of a sailing vessel (whether in the 15th or 20th century) is an extremely complicated technical profession in which most historians have only limited or superficial knowledge. I will show in this chapter (in layman's language) how this new empirical research is conducted and why it is superior to non-empirical research using computers with suspect or erroneous control data programmed into them. Then in Chapters 5 and 6, where I reconstructed Columbus' discovery and return voyages, I will show the demonstrated and mathematical proof that empirical field research is indeed the superior method.

Most previous artificial reconstruction and plotting of Columbus' voyage from his "diario" or log have been confined to the westbound discovery voyage with a view of determining the landfall island or supporting a previously selected island. These tracks while using the same basic navigational data from the log, have varied greatly from their termination or landfall because of the different input of the control data of postulated 1492 magnetic variation, possible leeway, and the estimated strength and direction of the ocean currents.

This study is not concerned solely with identifying the landfall island and will view the 1492 discovery voyage and the 1493 return voyage as a whole in order to determine the expertise of Columbus as an ocean navigator and the accuracy of his log. Since the 1493 return voyage has both a known departure point and a known termination or landfall point, it offers a stable navigational model to obtain and prove data that can then be applied with confidence to the 1492 discovery voyage. This study is primarily concerned with the two segments of the voyage from Gomera to landfall and from Samana Bay to Santa Maria because only in this portion of the log has Las Casas left the detailed navigational data largely intact.

In the remaining segment of the log which deals with the meandering track through the islands after landfall on Guanahani, the navigational data of the log has been either omitted or so severely abridged that a valid and accurate reconstruction of the track cannot be made with any degree of accuracy until it reaches the large and easily identifiable islands of Cuba and Hispaniola. Yet some of our finest scholars heroically try to reconstruct this troubled track based upon Columbus' exaggerated, allegorical, and romantically inspired description of the islands, augmented only by the scant navigational data remaining. And Columbus' limited observed navigational data during this period is further flawed by being interspersed with data arrived at by his interpretation (or misinterpretation) of the Indian guides directions.

Just the fact that so many intelligent scholars can read and interpret this part of the log and then come up with *nine different islands* should tell us something! Let's face it, this inadequate and nebulous part of the log will not give us the answer, so we must search elsewhere and that's exactly what this book does.

While it is difficult to reconstruct a definitive track through the islands from this part of the log, Columbus does at this point give us a fairly good geographical description of the island of Guanahani. Analysis of this geographical description of Guanahani with a comparison of the competing islands will be made in Chapter 7.

In the Atlantic crossings, Columbus was not compelled to fill the log with colorful descriptions of exotic islands and native Indians, so he stuck to straight forward and clear navigational data of compass courses and distances covered for each leg of the voyage. However this portion of the log does contain a few entries that are ambiguous or open to different interpretation. But these are confined to some of the shorter legs and can be resolved to the point where the overall accuracy of the log for this period is not degraded to any significant amount.

The reconstructed tracks of the 1992 discovery voyage and the 1993 return voyage were arrived at by using "Gooney Bird" as a research test vehicle and sailing through the same waters on each leg at the same speed and on the same compass heading as Columbus reported in his log. As just stated, this may sound like a relatively simple and easy task but it isn't. Now you will have to bear with me because the explanation of how I accomplished this task can become technical and tedious at times. But an understanding of this procedure is a necessary part of the overall understanding of how Columbus sailed and navigated his voyage and how I was able to duplicate it.

To accomplish this empirical reconstruction of the track, it was necessary to accurately establish the control factors affecting the compass headings and to determine the correct speed to be sailed on each leg. First let's consider the speed as this is the determining factor for the distance of each leg.

Use of an arbitrary factor for converting the leagues sailed (as reported in the log) to nautical miles was used by McElroy in his artificial reconstruction of the Columbus voyage for Samuel Eliot Morison's *Admiral of the Ocean Sea*. This arbitrary procedure forced the track to terminate at Morison's postulated landfall. This arbitrary figure was irrationally arrived at because the distance *through the water* reported by Columbus for each leg was considered as his distance *over the bottom* in plotting the track, and this was far from the case. This flawed rationale and methodology has been used by most theoretical navigators who do research in this field.

In my empirical reconstruction, I sailed the speed rather than the distance for each leg which then allowed the actual currents to determine the *true* length or distance of each leg *over the bottom* in nautical miles. This is the evidentially salient factor that guarantees the superiority of my empirical research over all artificial theoretical research in this area!

Columbus reported his distance sailed in miles or leagues (four miles) based upon his estimate of his speed in miles per hour. And this would be his speed through the water and not over the bottom, which he would have no way of knowing. And further, his estimate of speed in miles per hour would be based upon the length of the standard mile that he was using for his navigation.

I used a factor of 2.67 nautical miles to the league to compute the speed Columbus sailed each reported leg. This 2.67 nautical miles to the league control factor is based upon Columbus using the Mediterranean 5000 palm mile of 4060 feet to the nautical mile for his navigation. James E. Kelley Jr., first proposed this mile factor as the mile standard used by Columbus for his navigation in a paper contained in the, *Proceedings of the First San Salvador Conference*, in 1986. This control factor will be proven correct in my reconstructed tracks in Chapters 5 and 6. That takes care of the speed, now for the compass headings to be sailed.

The compass headings sailed for each leg were those from the log corrected for 1492/1493 magnetic variation (see Figure 16). These corrections were applied to the compass headings in the log based upon the premise that Columbus was using a compass with the north index set on magnetic north rather than true north at the city of manufacture. This premise is confirmed in the discussion of 1492/1493 magnetic variation which follows.

Corrections were also made for leeway where applicable. My stated opinion on the subject of leeway is that Columbus (or any other navigator using dead reckoning) was reporting (and plotting) the course the vessel made good for each leg (see Chapter 2) rather than the heading steered. Thus he would have automatically taken leeway into account so no correction is needed. Currently the only two knowledgeable and experienced ocean sailors involved in the study of Columbus's navigation are Robin Knox Johnston (the well known British singlehanded circumnavigator) and myself and we both agree on this salient point.

However, my theoretical navigator colleagues in this discipline feel strongly (and wrongly) that Columbus was so naive about the sailing characteristics of his vessels that he was unaware of the effect of leeway on his course. So to avoid their possible claim that my findings are flawed, I included this negligible leeway correction factor in my computations.

The analysis of both the 1492 discovery voyage and the 1493 return voyage (Chapters 5 and 6) confirms the fact that leeway is a negligible factor, but nevertheless this factor has been misused by some scholars to force their computer tracks to the desired landfall. Estimated leeway drift for different points of sail for Niña and Santa Maria were supplied by Charles Morgan Jr., a respected naval architect of sailing vessels.

While sailing these corrected compass headings through the same waters and at the same speed as Columbus, the resultant true track *over the bottom* in both distance and azimuth was then determined empirically by the actual currents.

To accomplish the same thing, a theoretical navigator must program the questionable estimated currents from a DMA pilot chart into his computer. I should explain that the Defense Mapping Agency (DMA) issues pilot charts of the North Atlantic annually giving the meteorological forecasts of average wind strength and direction, air temperature, and wave heights, for every month of the year. These charts also contain the average current strength and direction gathered from reports of shipping since the early part of the nineteenth century. The average current information on these charts is intended only for shipping companies to plan their ocean routes for minimal fuel consumption and in no way does it supply the *accurate and definitive* current information required to accurately reconstruct or plot Columbus' track.

I have shown the control factors necessary to apply in sailing "Gooney Bird" to reconstruct the track from the Columbus log. Now let's examine how this was physically done to provide an accurate and viable track across the Atlantic to determine Columbus' true landfall island and in turn determine the accuracy of his navigation and his log.

At first glance it might appear that a sailing vessel to duplicate the track of Columbus should be a square rigged wooden vessel of about the same size and shape as the Columbus vessels, but that is not at all the case. The basic requirement is for a submerged sailboat hull that will move through the same waters at the same speed and thus be acted upon by the currents to the same degree, and what the topsides (the hull above the waterline) and the sail plan looks like is completely irrelevant. In like manner, the submerged hull should have enough wetted surface (drag) to react to the currents to the same degree, and these factors cannot be judged by size alone.

The vessel used in this research is a Southern Cross, a heavy displacement, full keel, double-ended cutter from the board of Thomas Gilmer, a naval architect noted for his designs of traditional, seaworthy, deep water sailing vessels. This traditional hull form of a double-ender with outboard rudder (Niña and Santa Maria were double-enders with outboard rudder) dates back to the English Channel cutters of the 1800's which in turn were developed over the years from the English cog, a vessel contemporary with Columbus' caravels and naos.

While topsides, construction methods, and sail plans have changed drastically over the years, the underwater hull form of a traditional heavy displacement sailboat has changed very little since the 15th century or earlier. The Southern Cross hull has very nearly the same draft as Columbus' vessels and the full keel as opposed to the smaller keels of his vessels offers considerably more lateral effective wetted surface to be acted upon by cross currents. Figure 14 gives a graphic comparison of the underwater hull form of the Southern Cross and Niña and illustrates how the two vessels would react to ocean currents to the same degree. Thus my Southern Cross sailing vessel "Gooney Bird" will be carried along and react to the ocean currents to the same degree as Columbus' vessels in spite of their difference in size.

As I have indicated, it was necessary to sail "Gooney Bird" on the same (corrected) compass heading and at the same speed through the water as the Santa Maria and Niña and this normally was no problem since the practical hull speed of the three vessels is very close. However, since there is no way the wind speed and direction would be identical for each leg, I had to assist my sails with my engine when I could not reach the speed required due to my lighter sailing conditions. Conversely, when Columbus had light winds and

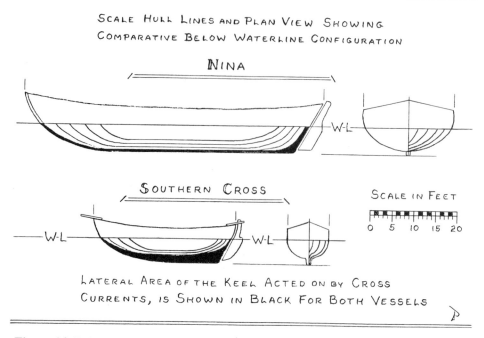

SCALE HULL LINES AND PLAN VIEW SHOWING
COMPARATIVE BELOW WATERLINE CONFIGURATION

NINA

W-L

SOUTHERN CROSS

SCALE IN FEET

W-L   W-L

0   5   10   15   20

LATERAL AREA OF THE KEEL ACTED ON BY CROSS
CURRENTS, IS SHOWN IN BLACK FOR BOTH VESSELS

Figure 14. Below water hull configuration of "Niña" and "Gooney Bird" (Southern Cross).

mine were strong, I reduced sails to slow to his speed. As noted above, the currents acting on the submerged hull do not know or care whether that hull is being driven by sail alone or a combination of sail and engine, nor do they care what the air temperature or the exact time of the year might be.

Another requirement of the research vessel is to be able to accurately collect and record the navigational data necessary for a valid and accurate plotting of the duplicated track. To accomplish this my research vessel "Gooney Bird" is specially constructed and customized for long ocean passages and has the latest state of the art navigation equipment installed. And "Gooney Bird" has one primary and three backup electronic autopilots that can accurately steer a given heading better than I can.

The methodology of using a sailing vessel to empirically duplicate the track of Columbus also requires that this vessel be acted upon by the same sea conditions that influenced and determined Columbus' track in his 1492-1493 voyage. Is that possible? The answer is yes!

The two conditions in the North Atlantic Ocean in 1492-1493 that affected the track of Columbus are the strength and direction of the ocean currents and the magnetic variation which prevailed at the time. Let's take these one at a time and start with the ocean currents.

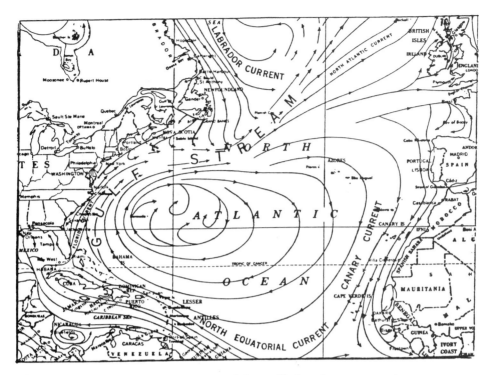

Figure 15. The North Atlantic Subtropical Gyre of induced ocean currents.

The crucial and significant effect of the ocean currents on the artificially plotted track is the weak point in other previous research which this study overcomes by using the actual currents rather than the postulated or estimated data from incomplete or suspect sources. It then follows that if the 1991 ocean currents are to be empirically used as a control factor, they should be the same as those existing in 1492-1493. Are they the same? The answer is again, yes!

The ocean currents are determined by the natural geophysical forces contained in the North Atlantic subtropical gyre. This North Atlantic clockwise gyre around a slightly mounded Sargasso Sea is set in motion and controlled by forces induced by gravity and the difference in temperature and density of the arctic and tropical waters, balanced against forces arising from the rotation of the earth in what fluid dynamicists call geostrophic circulation. These tremendous natural forces have not changed since Columbus' time so the currents resulting from these forces will also be unchanged.

I realize to say the currents have not changed is stating an absolute, which seldom if ever occurs in nature. Of course there have been certain climatic changes since Columbus' time, but the effect of these relatively small climatic changes on these tremendous inherent natural forces causing the mid ocean currents would be so small as to be negligible. With regard to any increase or decrease of the mean temperature of the atmosphere since Columbus' time, it should be borne in mind that it is the *difference* in temperature (and density) between the arctic and tropical waters that starts these currents on their way. This *difference* in temperature is quite independent of a change in the *mean* temperature, and so the currents are unaffected to any significant degree if the atmosphere has become warmer or cooler.

In like manner since I did not sail the two tracks on the exact calendar dates as Columbus, the seasonal changes of the North Atlantic gyre must also be considered. There is some seasonal change in the shape of the North Atlantic gyre, but this primarily affects the northern most (arctic) and the southern most (equatorial) extremes of the gyre and since both tracks passed through the central portion of the gyre, this seasonal difference would also be negligible.

The North Atlantic gyre and its peripheral currents is graphically shown in the chart in Figure 15 which is taken from an insert on a U.S. DMA Pilot Chart. The peripheral currents affecting Columbus' voyage are also shown in the chart and these will be discussed in the analysis of the 1492 and 1493 ocean tracks in Chapters 5 and 6.

Having established the fact that the currents affecting my track in 1991 were the same (within a reasonably insignificant amount) as those affecting Columbus in 1492-1493, let's now look at the other factor affecting the track. The magnetic variation for the North Atlantic Ocean for the 1492-1493 years is the other factor affecting the reconstruction of Columbus' voyage and this proved to be my thorniest problem.

Both John W. McElroy, who plotted the entire round trip of Columbus for Samuel Eliot Morison in 1941, and Luis Marden, who plotted the 1492 westbound discovery voyage (with aid of a computer) for the *National Geographic* magazine in 1986, used the Willem van Bemmelen isogonic lines to correct Columbus' reported compass headings in their plotted tracks. Isogonic lines on a nautical chart join points of equal magnetic variation. Willem van Bemmelen, a Dutch geophysicists furnished these postulated isogonic lines for the year 1500 in a paper published in 1899. These isogonic lines have subsequently been largely discredited and since my appeal for assistance in finding a better source to a large number of my colleagues working in this and related fields had gone unanswered, I developed my own isogonic lines for the years 1492-1493.

As with any problem solving technique, I took the known factors and extrapolated from them to solve for the unknown factors. These known factors were extracted from every available source document I could find including a diligent search of documents in the cartographical library of the British Museum where I was ably assisted by Dr. Helen Wallis (see Acknowledgements). The collected known factors for magnetic variation in the Columbus era are these:

A large area of strong westerly variation existed in the area just south of Newfoundland. John Cabot noted a two point (22.5 degrees) westerly variation near Newfoundland in his 1497 voyage. Also a strong westerly variation can be deduced from the clockwise tilting of the shores of Newfoundland in early maps; Cantino 1502, Reinel 1505, and Miller (1) 1525.

A 5.6 degree (1/2 point) easterly variation existed at Seville, a three degree easterly variation at Havana, and a small but undetermined westerly variation in the north and central Bahamas. These factors are from the published and unpublished research of James E. Kelley Jr., and furnished in private correspondence in 1989, 1990. (see bibliography)

A three degree easterly variation existed in the area of the Canary Islands. This factor was obtained from C. A. Schott's study of variation at the time of Columbus, published in 1881 (see bibliography).

Columbus' log also contains references from which we can deduce magnetic variation at two more points on the track across the Atlantic from Gomera:

On 13 September Columbus noted that at the beginning of night the compasses northwested and in the morning they northeasted. Columbus was observing the circular movement of Polaris around true north (about 3.6 degree radius in 1492) and the fact that the needle split north on both sides (east & west) indicates he was on a zero isogonic line.

This observation occurred at about 27 degrees longitude and 28 degrees latitude in an area where the easterly variation would have been decreasing from the 5.6 degrees in Seville through the three degrees in the Canaries. The observation at this point also confirms my premise that Columbus was using an uncorrected compass with the north index set on magnetic north, and not true north at the city of manufacture.

A zero or a very small variation in this same general area is also confirmed in Ferdinand's *Historie* where he summarized from Columbus' log of the second voyage. After reporting from the log that Columbus was quite certain they were a little west of the Azores, Ferdinand then reports Columbus as stating: "This morning the Flemish compass needles pointed a quarter north-west, as usual, and the Genoese, which generally agree with them, deviated very little." This not only substantiates my area of small variation in mid-ocean but quite firmly establishes the fact that Columbus did not rely on his Flemish compass (as asserted by Morison and others) but instead relied on his Genoese Compass which had the needle (and the north index) set on magnetic north.

In this regard, the treatise of Jean Rotz on 16th century magnetic variation (see bibliography) brings out the fact that while the Portuguese, French, Scots, English, and Flemish navigators all corrected for a variation of about north, a half quarter northeast, the Italian navigators sailing in the same waters made no correction at all to their compasses. This conviction of the Genoese navigators that the compass needed no correction is further borne out by Columbus' remarks in the log on 30 September. After a long dissertation on the fact that the north star moved slightly (in relation to the compass needle) during the night, he summed up his confidence in the uncorrected compass by stating: "... at nightfall the needles decline a point northeast, and at daybreak they are right on the (north) star, from which it appears that the star moves as the other stars and that the *needles always point truly.*"

Another pertinent fact revealed here is that Columbus was fully aware of magnetic variation but considered its effect on his course so small that he could (and did) ignore it. It also follows that the Genoese navigator named Columbus would rely on his uncorrected Genoese compass, yet I find numerous discussions from my colleagues in this discipline about how Columbus used a Flemish or Portuguese compass (and was unaware of the correction) to explain what they see as a problem with Columbus' reported compass headings.

The log entry for 17 September has been mistakenly used by some scholars to indicate a strong westerly variation at that point. Such is not the case but it does give us information that is useful in determining the 1492 variation in the North Atlantic along Columbus' track.

On that date, at the beginning of night, the Spanish pilots noted that the compasses northwested a full point (11.25 degrees) and became alarmed. At dawn the compasses were back on north, so it was a simple error on the part of the pilots, probably sighting on one of the guards instead of Polaris. The pilots never mentioned this (alleged) large westerly variation again so they obviously realized it was their mistake and the compass needle had not actually changed. This certainly cannot be used to indicate a westerly variation at that point, yet some of our academic theoretical navigators have turned out learned sounding (but flawed) computer studies using that non-existing large westerly variation. The really significant point about this log entry is that it shows the pilots became alarmed if variation approached 11 degrees.

And since the pilots or Columbus never became alarmed about excessive variation during the entire voyage after this incident, it would indicate that they never subsequently ran into variation approaching 11 degrees. Morison supports this sound logical reasoning in stating that; "although Columbus was aware of variation, it never really concerned him, since all his voyages were conducted in areas of small variation of less than six degrees."

Another log entry which relates to variation was on 30 September. This log entry has also been mistakenly interpreted as indicating a large westerly variation, but such is (again) not the case. On this date Columbus states: "When night comes the compasses northwest one quarter and when dawn comes they coincide with the north star exactly."

This must be read carefully. Once again he is merely observing the small movement of Polaris as it circles true north. He did not say the compass moved to the northwest one full degree, as most all Columbian scholars mistakenly assert. If he had meant that, he would have said that the compass moved to north, a quarter northwest (Norte vna quarta al norveste). Instead, he said they moved to the northwest one quarter (norueste an vna quarta). What he is saying here is the compass moved to the northwest one quarter of a point (2.8 degrees) then returned to north in the morning.

If indeed the compasses had moved a full point, the pilots would have become alarmed as they were on 17 September. So once again he is just noting the small circle that Polaris was making around true north. The fact that the compasses did not split true north by moving both northwest and northeast as on 13 September, and instead moved one quarter of a point only to the northwest would indicate that on 30 September (about latitude 26 north and longitude 51 west) he had entered an area of possibly two or three degree westerly variation.

This now gives me seven geographical points, scattered across the North Atlantic, in which the variation for the 1492/1493 time period is known. Placing these areas of known variation on a chart, I then joined them with an extrapolated geometric pattern of isogonic lines which follow the general pattern of the earth's magnetic field. The chart of isogonic lines thus developed is shown in Figure 16.

To summarize my findings as shown in Figure 16, we can see that Columbus would have started his voyage with only a small easterly variation, which gradually dropped to zero or a small negligible variation for over one third of the voyage in mid-ocean, then gradually changed to a small westerly variation in the Bahamas. However, there has been a plethora of Columbian scholars searching with chimerical passion for an area of large westerly variation somewhere on Columbus' track to support their particular theory. They will find that large westerly variation only in their own nebulous

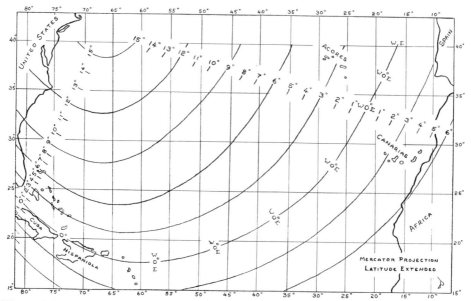

Figure 16. The isogonic lines showing magnetic variation of the North Atlantic for the years 1492-1493.

speculative computer deductions or through distorted misinterpretation of early documents, rather than in the hard cold facts of reality and logic.

I would hasten to say that in this limited study I make no claims to have identified where the north and south magnetic poles were located deep within the magma of the globe in 1492. I agree entirely with most geophysicists who affirm that this would be a virtually impossible task. However, my rational and logical research has been restricted to only a narrow part of the earth's globe for which I have sufficient data to arrive at only that magnetic variation experienced by Columbus.

Nevertheless I am faced with instant pseudo geophysicists who assert from their limited knowledge of the subject that I could not possibly have accomplished this task. I have yet to see a rational and supported argument showing how my findings are in error. Instead I have heard only unsupported assertions that what I have done cannot be done. Really now!

The magnetic variation depicted in Figure 16 was used as the basis for correcting the compass headings for each leg in the log, and this correction together with sailing through the unchanged currents gives the assurance that my research in 1991 was conducted in the same sea conditions that affected the track of Columbus' vessels in 1492-1493.

⚓ ⚓ ⚓ ⚓ ⚓ ⚓ ⚓ ⚓

I've told you a little about my sailboat "Gooney Bird" but only to establish its hull form and characteristics as suitable for the task of accurately duplicating Columbus' voyage. Perhaps now I should tell you a little more about "Gooney Bird" as she was a vital part of this research effort and performed her task well.

I'll start with the name. Gooney Bird is not some whimsical name I picked out of the air although it may sound that way. Gooney Bird is the nickname for the revered and dependable military C-47 (or Douglas DC-3) transport airplane that I flew on many occasions back when I was a pilot in the Army Air Corps and later USAF. Also Gooney Bird is the nickname for the Wake Island albatross, a beautiful large sea bird that ranges for long distances over the oceans of the world. So my sailing vessel "Gooney Bird" has a most appropriate and proud name that fits her well.

I built "Gooney Bird" from a bare fiberglass hull and deck that I purchased from the C. E. Ryder company in Bristol, Rhode Island. I chose to go this route so I could customize it for the long ocean passages I had in mind. This was no easy task and it took me 2½ years of working 10-12 hours a day, 7 days a week, to finish the job. The hull and rigging are beefed up considerably to take the sometimes punishing seas and weather of the North Atlantic. I am also able to carry more than normal fuel, water, and stores, allowing me to stay at sea for the long periods necessary in my research duplicating the long voyages of Ponce de León and Columbus.

I'm a singlehander, so I have designed the standing and running rigging so I can easily and safely handle the sails and other equipment by myself. And that fact is what decided the size of the boat. It is large enough to be seaworthy and comfortable, yet small enough to be handled by one man.

I have said that I customized "Gooney Bird" in order to "duplicate" the long voyages of Ponce de León and Columbus. But believe me, I'm duplicating only the navigation track or path that they sailed and not trying to duplicate the rather Spartan life the Spaniards lived aboard their vessels.

I use a three burner propane stove with an oven and broiler instead of cooking in an iron pot over a wood fire burning in a sand box on deck. My meat products are from cans rather than slaughtering livestock as I go. Most of my fish also comes from cans (I'm big on sardines and smoked herring), but I do occasionally put a fishing line over the side which I'm sure Columbus' crew did constantly. My one concession to perhaps more closely duplicate their life style is that I don't have refrigeration or ice aboard so I have to drink my rum "neat" as the English sailor would say.

Figure 17. The sailing yacht "Gooney Bird" in which the author re-sailed and duplicated the voyages of Columbus and Ponce de León.

I also have much more creature comfort and safety equipment than Columbus had, supplied primarily by an ample supply of 12 volt marine deep-cycle batteries. I keep my three large batteries well charged by running the diesel engine (with its 55 amp alternator) only 2-3 hours a day. From these I can keep the boat well lit at night and can run my electronic autopilots, radios, and navigation equipment. In the way of radios I have an RDF, EPIRB, VHF, and SSB. The single sideband radio (SSB) is a powerful full band radio that I can transmit and receive in a range that goes half way around the world. For navigation I have Loran-C, Sat-Nav, GPS, RDF, Depthometer, knotmeter (includes a log and water temperature), and a Weather-Fax. The Weather-Fax gives me an up to date weather map of the entire North Atlantic. In my 1992 voyage I was able to follow hurricane "Andrew" as it moved across my path (luckily about 700 miles away) to its destructive path through south Miami.

I must hasten to say that with all that sophisticated electronic navigation equipment aboard, I used only my magnetic compass and knotmeter to duplicate Columbus' voyage because that is all he used to sail his vessel. I must admit I cheated a bit here as Columbus estimated his speed, but I'm not as good as Columbus at that task so I used my electronic knotmeter to stick to his speed. My sophisticated navigation equipment was then used only to record the exact over-the-bottom track that I (and Columbus) was making by following just that compass heading and speed.

I also have a stereo system aboard with six inch speakers in which I can play my collection of over 100 tapes when I'm out of reach of shore stations. Columbus didn't have anything like that but he and all the early voyagers of this period had sailors aboard who played their flutes, drums, and string instruments for the entertainment of the ship on those long days at sea. At one point on Columbus' third voyage when he had some friendly Indian canoes gathered around the boat, Columbus thought he would entertain them so he ordered his musicians to strike up a tune. This was a bad move which he never repeated as the Indians thought it was a war dance and fired off an avalanche of arrows and fled.

I said I am a singlehander but I'm not exactly alone on the boat. I have a gray female tabby named "Hooker" who is the official "Ship's Cat." "Hooker" came aboard nine years ago when I was in Galveston, Texas for a singlehanded race across the Gulf of Mexico to the St. Petersburg Yacht Club. She was just a small underfed stray kitten and she had decided rather firmly that she was going to live aboard "Gooney Bird" even though there were many larger and more magnificent boats all around me. After unsuccessfully throwing her off the boat several times, I gave up and bought a litter box and some cat food and she has been living aboard ever since.

Hooker is no help at all in running the boat, the only thing she contributes is her presence, and I really think she believes she owns the boat and my sole purpose on the boat is to keep her food dish filled. She eats primarily the dried cat food that comes in bags with an occasional treat of canned fish cat food. She then supplements this diet with flying fish that she gathers up off the deck as they come aboard at night.

To begin my return voyage reconstruction in 1991, my first task was to get "Gooney Bird" from my home port in Bradenton, Florida to Columbus' starting point in Samana Bay at the eastern end of the Dominican Republic. This proved to be the hardest part of the entire voyage as I had to beat into the east and southeast trade winds for well over 1000 miles. I passed through the Keys at Channel Five near Key Largo, then getting on the Great Bahama Bank west of Andros Island, I sailed south and anchored in the lee of the Ragged Islands to await more favorable winds.

My anchorage was on the "Columbus Bank," so named because Columbus passed the Ragged Islands (he named them "Sand Islands") on his way to Cuba in 1492. I had anchored in this same spot the year before on my way to Ponce de León's starting point in Puerto Rico and had to wait five days for favorable winds. This time I was luckier and the next day the winds diminished and came more easterly so I sailed on through the Turks and Caicos Islands and reached Samana Bay in about five days.

Columbus anchored near the mouth of Samana Bay at a point he named Punta de las Fleches (point of the arrows) because unlike his previous friendly reception by the Indians, here he was met with hostility and arrows. The area hasn't changed much because with the extreme poverty and high unemployment rate, the main occupation of the inhabitants seems to be robbing American tourists and yachtsmen, frequently at the point of a sharp machete.

It was at this point that Columbus started his log for his return voyage to Spain in early 1493 and so it was my starting point in 1991 for my research voyage to reconstruct his track to Santa Maria in the Azores, covered in Chapter 5 following.

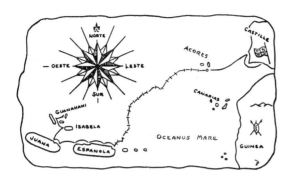

5

Analysis of the Return Voyage to Spain in 1493

This portion of the return voyage from Samana Bay (Hispaniola) to Santa Maria (Azores) was sailed and reconstructed first because it contains both a known departure point and a known termination point thus providing a stable model upon which to prove or correct my postulated control factors. Re-sailing this return voyage proved to be much harder than the westbound discovery voyage and just a glance at the chart will show you why. The westbound voyage contained very few changes in heading since Columbus was set on sailing due west and with favorable following winds only changed that when the few conditions forced him to. However, the winds on the return voyage were anything but favorable, causing many changes in heading and speed which I had to duplicate.

On the return voyage, Columbus left Samana Bay, Hispaniola (Punta de las Fleches) on 16 January 1493, to continue his exploring to the island of Carib (Puerto Rico) and the island of Matinino (probably St. Croix). After sailing 13 hours, he ran into a strong southeasterly wind which was contrary for where he was headed but favorable for going to Spain so he turned to a heading of northeast by east and headed for home. Columbus in reporting his course as northeast by east was simply stating this was the most easterly course the trade winds would allow, and not necessarily naming that as the direct course to Spain.

After leaving Samana Bay, Columbus no longer filled the log with his verbose and colorful descriptions of the islands exotic flora and fauna and native Indians, so Las Casas was able to leave his detailed dead reckoning navigation data of compass headings and distances largely intact. At this time, Columbus decided for reasons known only to himself, to report his navigation day from sunset to sunset with a 13 hour night and an 11 hour day.

Columbus used a 12 hour day and a 12 hour night for his 1492 westbound navigation which would be compatible with his four hour watches. I believe Columbus at this time may very well have adhered to a standard 12 hour night shift and taking his day end readings at 1800 for his navigation day. Then because Columbus noted the time of sunrise and sunset in his remarks, Las Casas (not being a navigator) assumed that was when he started and ended his navigation day. The question is moot for the purpose of my reconstruction since the 24 hour time and distance would be the same.

Most of the log entries are straight forward and easily understood, enabling an accurate reconstruction of each leg of the track. The log entry for 16 January (day 1) is one exception since it gives the compass heading and distance for each leg but not the time. The log reads that Columbus departed Samana Bay at three hours before dawn, sailed four legs with varying wind conditions for a total of 42 leagues or 112 nautical miles in the 15 hours before sunset where he ended his navigation day. This computes out to an average speed of 7.5 knots which is completely unreasonable for the wind conditions he must have encountered.

He departed with a land breeze which is never very strong, then encountered a west wind which is unusual in this area of predominant easterly trade winds and when they do occur are never very strong. Then later in the day he had to trim sails in order to head southeast to the island of Carib and since a square rigged vessel is notoriously slow when hard on the wind, he could not possibly reach that speed of 7.5 knots. Following this he stated "the wind freshened", which would indicate that prior to this time the wind had not been fresh or strong.

I can only conclude that Columbus must have sailed that 112 nautical miles in a longer time period than the 15 hours indicated in the log. The logical explanation is that the log entry reading: "He departed three hours before daybreak", is a transcription error and should read: "He departed three hours before day end" (of the previous day). This would put 27 hours in day 1 navigation period which would compute out to an average speed of 4.2 knots, a completely reasonable speed for those wind conditions. This would also explain why Columbus, having started his navigation on day 1 from sunset to sunset, elected to continue that unusual procedure for the remainder of the voyage.

Columbus would have meticulously plotted the compass course and distance for each leg of his voyage on his portolan chart (see Figure 6) in order to fix his position. Since he did not compensate for the effect of variation on his compass heading and was unaware of the effect of the currents on both the

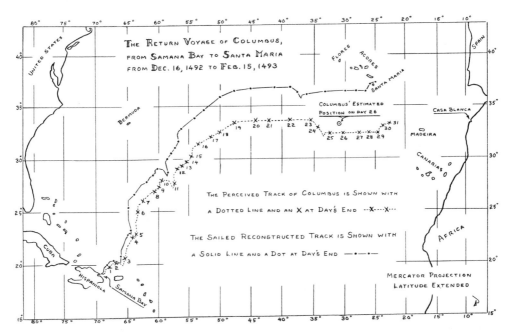

Figure 18. The perceived and actual track of Columbus from Samana Bay to Santa Maria.

distance and azimuth of each leg, then for Columbus this plotted track would represent what he thought or perceived as his true course and position *over the bottom*. Columbus "perceived" and fully believed this plotted course was true and correct but it was far from it, and the reason and degree for this error will be shown later. This dead reckoning track Columbus would have plotted is shown on the chart in Figure 18 and labeled his "perceived" track.

Analysis of this track reveals several instances that confirms Columbus as a masterful and accurate dead reckoning navigator. To maintain an accurate dead reckoning course, each change of either heading or speed must be logged and plotted as a separate leg. Columbus certainly did just that! There are 84 separate legs occasioned by either a heading or speed change. Even during the tremendous storm near the end of the voyage, Columbus faithfully logged changes of only a few hours.

The effectiveness of this meticulous plotting can be seen in the accuracy of Columbus' position report given on 10 February (day 26) when he stated he was south of Flores and west of Nafe (Casa Blanca). I have plotted this position on the chart in Figure 18 and you will note that it falls about three fourths of the way through day 26 which would be mid day or about when he would be making this estimate. Note also that it is indeed south of Flores and west of Nafe (Casa Blanca).

Later in this analysis it will be shown that the positive and negative currents affecting his distance over the bottom canceled out so this would also be a true position related to distance. This indicates that his computation on distance based on his estimate of speed through the water is extremely accurate to be this close after 26 days of a complicated track involving many changes in both heading and speed. And let me caution the reader that this position on day 26 is where Columbus' dead reckoning indicated he should be, not where he actually was.

But what can we say about his azimuth (latitude) position? His actual position is 70 nautical miles north of his perceived position. Here we must remember that my plot of Columbus' dead reckoning plot was started at the exact (modern chart) latitude of Samana Bay, while we do not know the chart latitude at which Columbus started his plot. In like manner, my plot of his estimated position is also based upon the exact (modern chart) latitude of Casa Blanca (Nafe), while we do not know how accurately the latitude was depicted on his portolan chart. For these reasons we can draw no definite conclusion on the azimuth accuracy of the plot like we can on the distance.

On 3 February (day 19) Columbus eyeballed Polaris and declared it was very high as at Cabo de San Vicente (southwest cape of Portugal) and tried to use the quadrant or astrolabe but was unable to do so because of the waves. Columbus was at latitude 35 degrees, 45 minutes north on this day, which is about 75 nautical miles south of the latitude of Cabo de San Vicente. Not bad for an eyeball sight, but Columbus apparently didn't trust it because seven days later after sailing largely east (at the same latitude) he went back to his dead reckoning (the perceived track) when he reported himself west of Nafe which placed him over 200 miles south of Cabo de San Vicente. This clearly shows that Columbus was a confirmed dead reckoning navigator, having little faith in his infrequent celestial sightings.

On 6 February (day 22) Columbus reported that he made 10 miles per hour at night and 11 miles per hour during the day. This is one of the log entries that advocates of Columbus overestimating his speed use to prove their point by saying that Niña was incapable of that high speed.

Let's look at that 11 miles per hour and see if Niña could reach it. Columbus was not reporting 11 statute miles per hour, or 11 nautical miles per hour (knots), or 11 Roman miles per hour, instead he was reporting 11 of his Mediterranean (5000 palms) miles per hour. He made 38.5 leagues in 11 hours at that speed which at 2.67 nautical miles to the league (based on Columbus' mile) comes to 102.8 nautical miles in eleven hours, computing out to 9.3 knots.

With a waterline length of nearly 60 feet, Niña would have a theoretical hull speed of between 8 and 9 knots and with the sailing conditions of that day of strong steady westerlies and a following sea, could easily reach the 9.3 knots reported by Columbus. I might explain that theoretical hull speed is that optimum speed at which it can be driven with minimum force applied. Under ideal conditions this speed can be exceeded by 15 to 20 percent.

Those who would say that Niña could not reach that high speed also cite the fact that Niña's hull was probably foul with weed and barnacles. This is probably true, but the theoretical hull speed is dependant entirely on the waterline length and hull shape, without regard to the smoothness of the bottom. The vessel is capable of reaching that speed if enough force (wind) is applied, so this simply means that a vessel with a foul bottom requires more wind to reach its hull speed than it would with a clean bottom. And Niña in those strong westerlies in those high latitudes would have had more than enough wind to overcome that foul bottom and reach (or exceed) its hull speed. So to emphasize the point made here and elsewhere in this study, Columbus was very accurate in estimating his speed and this log entry does not indicate that he overestimated his speed.

In sailing "Gooney Bird" dead downwind in these same strong sustained westerlies in this part of the North Atlantic, I have frequently reached 9 and 9.5 knots for days on end. And the hull speed of "Gooney Bird" (6 knots) is far less than that of Niña. But when I cite this experience to my colleagues in this discipline, they shrug it off and go back to quoting their theoretical figures from a textbook and say that Columbus must be wrong in his estimate of speed because they can prove that Niña couldn't do it. This reminds me of my college days when my aeronautics professor showed how the theoretical data and formulae (body weight and mass vs plane area of wings) from textbooks could be used to prove that a bumblebee could not possibly fly.

I might add that I don't really like to go that fast in "Gooney Bird" because it means the boat is very close to being overpowered and to go on deck to reduce sails in these conditions can be rather unpleasant. But my "Autohelm 2000" autopilot has proved itself fully capable of handling the tiller under these extreme conditions, never allowing "Gooney Bird" to approach a broaching condition. A "broach" is when rudder control is lost and the boat suddenly swerves sideways to the wind and waves which can end up in a disastrous knockdown or capsize.

"Gooney Bird's" stability under these potentially dangerous conditions can be attributed to its long fixed keel trailed by an oversized outboard rudder. Figure 14 shows how both "Niña" and "Gooney Bird" share this same hull design feature which makes for fast safe downwind sailing in the strong westerly winds of the North Atlantic.

There are those who insist that the Spanish seamen and navigators

Figure 19. "Gooney Bird" about 300 miles west of Santa Maria running before the strong North Atlantic westerlies in 20 ft. seas. Columbus encountered similar conditions in this same area in his 1493 return voyage in "Niña." Looking aft from the foredeck, the "Autohelm" autopilot is steering.

(pilots) were every bit as good as Columbus and so could have accomplished the mission without him. The accuracy of Columbus' navigation over that of the several Spanish pilots aboard was confirmed on 15 February (day 31) when they sighted Santa Maria. Previous to that day Columbus said they were south of Flores, while the other pilots aboard; Vicente Yañez Pinzón, Sancho Ruyz, Pero Alonzo Nino, and Roldan, all charted their positions and all said they were in the vicinity of Madeira. Las Casas in addressing this situation in the log states: "So that they (the Spanish pilots) were nearer Castille than the Admiral by 150 leagues (600 miles). He (Columbus) says that when, through God's grace, they see land, it will be known who figured most correctly." And when they did see land (Santa Maria) five days later, it was Columbus who had "figured most correctly" and it was the four Spanish pilots who had overestimated their speed and so distance to a considerable degree, and not Columbus who was right on the money.

Another example of the superiority of Columbus' navigation over that of the Spanish pilots occurs in the log of 8 August when they were looking for the island of Lanzarote after a 600 mile passage from Palos. Las Casas has this to say: "There were among the pilots of the three caravels diverse opinions about where they were, and the Admiral (Columbus) came out nearest the truth." All this merely emphasizes the point I made in Chapter 2 of the proven superiority of Genoese trained navigators over those of the other European countries.

My empirical reconstruction of the 1493 return voyage is also shown in Figure 17 and labeled; "The Sailed Reconstructed Track." This is the "Perceived Track" of Columbus when corrected for the effect of 1493 magnetic variation, leeway, and (empirically) the ocean currents during my reconstruction voyage.

As you can see, the reconstructed track for the first one third of the voyage was forced north and west from the "perceived track". This is primarily due to the Antilles current since this is in an area of small magnetic variation and the small leeway corrections intermittently came from both sides of the track, roughly canceling out. This strong Antilles current is an offshoot of the South Equatorial Current that joins the Florida Current north of the Bahamas to become the Gulf Stream. (See Figure 15)

In the middle one third of the voyage the track enters the area of light and variable currents in the Sargasso Sea and is forced west and north by the increasing westerly magnetic variation rather than the currents.

Then in the last one third of the voyage, the track has entered the edge of the Gulf Stream and the distance of each leg is increased by the following current while the azimuth of the track is still being forced north by the stronger 1493 westerly magnetic variation. The track at this point was not in the axis or strong part of the Gulf Stream (3+ knots) but well south and east of the axis and it's attendant cold and warm water eddies, and in an area of small largely easterly flow.

The reconstructed track terminated at 37 degrees, 15 minutes north latitude and 24 degrees, 45 minutes west longitude which is about 35 nautical miles east northeast of Santa Maria.

Ideally, if all my postulated control factors had been exactly (and with no allowable tolerance) correct, I would have hit Santa Maria right on the nose just like Columbus but as it was, my termination point is just a little over one percentage point off. And since this 99 percent accuracy is well within reasonable tolerance for this type of research, I certainly confirmed that my postulated control factors are accurate. And the fact of the matter is, my track could well be closer than that one percentage point because while I passed north of Santa Maria, I was well within sight of it shortly before the termination of my track.

Analysis of the navigational data gathered during reconstruction of the return voyage reveals the following facts:

The total length of the reconstructed track was 2920 nautical miles and when the 35 nautical mile overrun is subtracted, makes the actual length of Columbus' voyage 2885 nautical miles over the bottom. Columbus reported the distance as 1085 leagues or 2897 nautical miles (through the water) a difference of 12 nautical miles.

This 12 nautical mile difference is misleading, as some of the 24 hour legs by themselves had over a 12 nautical mile difference. The 12 nautical mile difference in this instance is a total, indicating that of the many legs influenced in distance by the currents, the positive and negative effect on the distance was very nearly equal.

The azimuth displacement of the track by the currents would also affect the distance but to such a small degree as to be negligible for my analytical computations.

Thus the negligible modifying effect of the current on Columbus' estimate of distance allows the following analytical computation to determine the number of nautical miles in the league Columbus was using for his navigation:

The actual track of 2885 nautical miles divided by the 1085 leagues reported by Columbus equals 2.66 nautical miles to the league that Columbus was using for his navigation and upon which he based his estimate of speed and so distance. This provides irrefutable mathematical evidence that Columbus was using the Mediterranean 5000 palm mile of 2.67 nautical miles to the league (a difference of only 0.01 mile).

Further on this same thesis, if either the Portuguese Maritime league or the Spanish league factor of about 3.20 nautical miles to the league had been used as a controlling factor for determining speed and distance, the track instead of ending at Santa Maria (where we know it did) would have been 3472 nautical miles long and bypassed Santa Maria ending 587 miles beyond.

The Portuguese Maritime league which is used in this computation is based on the Roman mile of 4850 feet which computes out to 3.19 nautical miles to the league. The length of the Spanish mile or league is in dispute by Columbian scholars. Figures for nautical mile to the league range from 2.82 to 3.40. I have used 3.20 nautical miles to the league as an arbitrary average of these figures in the foregoing computation just to prove my point. These large and erroneous factors are used by most Columbian Scholars (even Morison) in their research, and of course results in their being forced to insist that Columbus grossly overestimated his speed.

I must hasten to explain here that my thesis shows and proves only that Columbus used his Genoese 5000 palm mile for navigation on the *first voyage* of 1492-1493. There is every indication that Columbus tired of the constant mathematical exercise of relating his Genoese navigational league to the longer Spanish league (which he referred to as the "Great League") used by the numerous Spanish pilots in the fleet, and so in the 2nd, 3rd, and 4th voyages reported his distances in the longer Spanish league. The letter of Dr. Chanca giving details of the second voyage would confirm this when he reported that Puerto Rico (Borinquen) was 30 leagues in length which at 90 nautical miles would very closely fit the Spanish league length of about 3.20 nautical miles.

With my control factors of Columbus' speed (from his 5000 palm mile), and the postulated magnetic variation for 1492-1493 confirmed by my reconstruction of the 1493 return voyage, I now felt confident to use these proven control factors in my reconstruction of the 1492 discovery voyage.

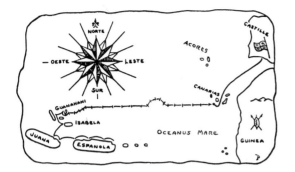

6

Analysis of the 1492 Discovery Voyage from Gomera to Landfall

Columbus departed Gomera on 6 September 1492 and was becalmed through 7 September between Gomera and Tenerife. The log indicates that on 8 September he had light winds but does not mention any movement. At three hours past midnight a strong wind came up from the northeast and he picked up his avowed heading of west to the Indies. I have postulated that Columbus in the light winds on 8 September would have worked his way south and west from between Gomera and Tenerife and was south of Gomera when the wind came up and he was able to start west.

It is at this point that Columbus would have started his dead reckoning navigation, and so at that point I started my reconstruction of his track across the Atlantic.

Columbus would have had a portolan chart showing the southern coast of Spain and Portugal, the African coast, and the islands of the Azores, Madeira, the Canaries, and Cape Verde, and the rest left blank for plotting his dead reckoning course to the Indies. When he finally finished plotting his course, the complete chart would look something like the chart in Figure 7.

Columbus was unaware of the effect of the currents and did not compensate for magnetic variation on his track, so he would have plotted each leg of the course (erroneously) as a true course and true distance *over the bottom.* I have plotted the track just as Columbus would have plotted it on his chart in Figure 7 and labeled it: "The Perceived Track of Columbus." My plot of this track is shown in Figure 20.

Columbus had learned from Toscanelli that Cipangu (Japan) and the Indies lay due west from the Canaries so he religiously stuck to that heading except in the middle of the voyage when head winds from a rare weak cold

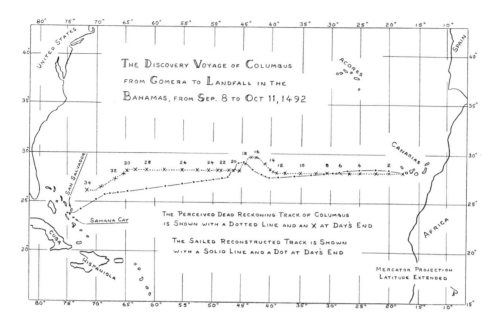

Figure 20. The perceived and actual track of the discovery voyage of Columbus in 1492.

front forced him off to the north. Then later he deviated briefly to the southwest, first when they mistook a cloudbank for land and later near the end when he followed flocks of birds that he believed were leading him to land.

Notice that his perceived dead reckoning track terminating at landfall on Guanahani was at latitude 26 degrees, 05 minutes north, far north of his actual landfall and out in the Atlantic far short of landfall on any island. But since Columbus was unaware of how the currents and magnetic variation had affected his track, this is where he thought Guanahani was located, so all of his subsequent dead reckoning would be from this point and thus would place the next islands he discovered too far north and too far to the east.

This northerly latitude error initiated by Columbus was to affect cartography of the New World for nearly a century following, where we find most islands and landmarks shown are one, two, or even three degrees too far north. In both my essay and my book on the voyage of Ponce de León (see bibliography) I pointed out and documented how this salient point had influenced the latitudes reported by Antón de Alaminos (Ponce de León's pilot) in the 1513 voyage.

The log of 13 October while at Guanahani also indicates this false impression he had of his latitude when commenting on the bronze skin coloration of the Indians he said: "Nor should anything else be expected since this island is on an east-west line with the island of Hierro in the Canaries."

This general remark in the narrative part of the log was not intended as a precise navigation fix (although some historians mistakenly use it as such) but it does indicate that Columbus from his dead reckoning plot, thought he was further north than he really was.

Another example that his dead reckoning plot placed him too far north is in a letter to the sovereigns following his return when he stated that Juana (Cuba) and Española were at 26 degrees north latitude (based upon his dead reckoning from Guanahani) when they are actually between 20 and 21 degrees north latitude.

My empirical reconstructed track of the discovery voyage is also shown on the chart in Figure 6 and labeled: "The Sailed Reconstructed Track". This is the "Perceived track" of Columbus when corrected for the effect of 1492 magnetic variation, leeway, and (empirically) for the ocean currents during my reconstruction voyage.

The reconstructed track trends north of Columbus' perceived track until day 8 when the two tracks touch. This initial northward trend is due to application of the easterly magnetic variation correction and would have been more pronounced but for the opposing influence of the southwesterly flowing Canary Current, a peripheral current of the North Atlantic gyre. Later in the voyage the reconstructed track trends south of the perceived track because of the application of the increasing westerly magnetic variation for which Columbus made no correction.

From about day 9 to day 27 the track is carried along in distance by the North Equatorial Current and you will notice each day I gained between 7-12 miles because of the easterly flowing current. Columbus was of course gaining this same 7-12 miles each day but he wasn't aware of it, which explains why his actual distance covered was greater than his estimate in the log. This *simple and elementary navigational fact*, so easily understood by any *trained and experienced navigator*, cannot be understood by most historians who come up with all manner of esoteric explanations for that difference in distance in the log. Their explanations for this difference ranges from Columbus' gross inability to estimate his speed and distance, to preposterous theories about how he was trying to conceal the truth from the Spanish pilots (which in turn brings on the equally preposterous theory of the second or secret log) so only he could find his way back to the Indies.

In the latter part of the voyage from about day 28 to landfall, the track comes under the influence of the strong Antilles Current which pushes the track in a northwesterly direction opposing the increasing westerly magnetic variation which tends to force the track south. This is the same current that forced the reconstructed return voyage north and west in this same area.

A good example of the significant controlling influence of this current is the 13 hour leg at the end of day 30 when I was steering 240.5 degrees but I made 270 degrees over the bottom. This nearly 30 degree (29.5) difference between the heading steered and the course made good (over the bottom) amply demonstrates how the ocean currents are the *primary* controlling factors rather than the lessr magnetic variation (or the non-existent leeway) factors.

Here I will pause for a moment and ask the reader to consider my thesis that empirical reconstruction of the voyage by a sailing vessel is superior to plotting the same track with a computer.

A review of the last few paragraphs will show how "Gooney Bird" was being sailed on a compass heading that was constantly changing (or more properly corrected) by an interplay between my postulated 16th century magnetic variation and the 20th century magnetic variation on my modern chart. Then in addition to this constant correction of the heading, the track was also being influenced by ocean currents that were constantly changing in direction and speed. And bear in mind that these changes were occurring constantly every hour in the 792 hours of the voyage. It should be obvious to even someone with only rudimentary knowledge of computer programming that to program all these constantly changing (with some being unknown or estimated) controlling factors into a computer would be a virtually impossible task. But to an *experienced ocean navigator with a well equipped sailing vessel* this is all in the day's work that is done every day to produce a controlled navigation track. So I must repeat that my empirical reconstruction of Columbus' track is superior to that produced by theoretical navigators bending over a computer!

The track ended at 23 degrees, 45.5 minutes north latitude, and 75 degrees, 11.0 minutes west longitude, passing within a few miles of the south cape of San Salvador and ended a few miles beyond. Termination of the track at this point would clearly support San Salvador as the landfall island, particularly when considered together with my 1987 reconstruction of the discovery voyage which also pointed to San Salvador as the landfall.

As in the return voyage reconstruction where my termination was at Santa Maria, I did not hit San Salvador right on, but was within the same one percentage point of Columbus' actual track. Here I should remind the reader that this 99 percent accuracy is not unique to Columbus. Earlier (Chapter 2) I reported that the 16th century historian Andres Bernaldez confirmed this 99 percent accuracy for experienced pilots of the Columbian era when he stated: "No one considers himself a good pilot and master who, ... makes an error of 10 leagues even in a crossing of 1000 leagues."

Figure 21. A romanticized depiction of Columbus' landing ceremony on Guanahani by Leopold Flameng in an 1878 French book on the voyage of Columbus.

It is interesting to note that while my return voyage track was slightly north of Santa Maria, the track of the 1492 discovery voyage was slightly south of San Salvador. This would lend support to my hypothesis that the small variance in azimuth of the tracks was due to a small (and insignificant) error in the amount of my postulated westerly variation.

In the 1493 return voyage, the positive and negative effect of the current on the distance was very nearly equal. However in the 1492 westbound voyage the currents had a positive or helping effect for about 80% of the time, amounting to an average of 0.25 knot help from the current for the entire voyage. As previously stated this *elementary navigational fact* clearly explains why Columbus' actual distance covered was greater than his estimate in the log. But it is this simple fact, so easily understood by an experienced ocean navigator, that has been grossly misinterpreted by historians with little or no real practical knowledge of navigation.

In mid-ocean in the easterly flowing North Equatorial Current he was helped along the way between 0.3 to 0.6 knots. This very closely computes out to the distance to be made up for the shortfall of the perceived track, once again substantiating the fact that Columbus was using the shorter Mediterranean mile (2.67 nautical miles to the league) for his navigation.

If the larger Portuguese Maritime League or the Spanish League factor (about 3.20) had been used in this reconstruction, the track would have ended 585 nautical miles beyond the Bahamas in the Gulf of Mexico 35 miles beyond the west coast of Florida. Yet the advocates of this larger mile factor explain this gross anomaly by doggedly insisting that Columbus grossly overestimated his speed and so his distance.

My empirical reconstruction of the 1492-1493 voyage as presented here and in the preceding chapters 4 & 5 have scientifically and mathematically proved that Columbus was an accurate dead reckoning navigator and that the log of his Atlantic track (and thus his chart of the Atlantic course to the islands and Española) was accurate. The accuracy of his lost chart to the Indies can be further confirmed by the successful completion of his subsequent voyages and the numerous re-supply voyages to Española by other contemporary navigators using his chart.

While Columbus was still away on his second voyage, his brother Bartolome was given three re-supply caravels which he sailed from an unnamed Andalusion port (probably Cadiz) in 1494 and arrived safely at Isabela in mid-summer. He undoubtably was supplied with a copy of Columbus' 1492 Atlantic chart which he was able to follow with accuracy to his destination. This voyage (and the 396 others to follow, see Chapter 2) confirms both the accuracy of Columbus' dead reckoning chart and the reliability of 15th century dead reckoning with the 32 point compass then in use.

Another example of Columbus' expertise and accuracy in dead reckoning navigation is in the report of his return to Spain following his second voyage. On his return from Española in 1496, Columbus hit Cape St Vicente only 35 miles north and only about 12 hours (1/2 day) after he had predicted. This once again confirmed his accuracy as a dead reckoning navigator and the accuracy of his Atlantic chart.

And of course the navigational feat most often cited by Humbolt, Charcot, Morison and other historians to substantiate Columbus as a superbly accurate dead reckoning navigator is his long over-water passage on the third voyage from Margarita to Española. On this voyage his last known departure landmark was the Cape Verde Islands after which he sailed thousands of miles through the doldrums to Trinidad then hundreds of miles in a meandering course along the northern coast of South America, and then he was able to accurately set a course of northwest by north for Española which he had left three years earlier. This feat could only have been accomplished by meticulously and accurately plotting each leg of the voyage which involved many changes of compass course and speed (distance) as he did during his 1492-1493 voyage as reported in Chapters 5 & 6 (ie: accurate dead reckoning navigation).

True this northwest by north course carried him 100 miles west of his destination on Española but this was due to the westerly flowing currents in the Caribbean of which Columbus at this time was unaware. Columbus at first could not understand why he had missed his mark as Las Casas reports: "Pesole de haber tanto decavdo," it weighed heavily on him to have fallen off so much. Then later Las Casas quotes Columbus who explained his miscalculation (quite correctly) by noting, "...the currents, which are here very strong, setting toward Terrae Firma and the west."

We do not have detailed navigational data for this part of the voyage so cannot assign a mathematical degree of accuracy to that northwest by north course as is possible in his 1492-1493, and 1496 voyages. For this reason I do not consider this as strong an argument for the accuracy of his navigation as my reconstructions and the several preceding examples. Nevertheless there are certainly enough facts known in this instance to establish it as one more confirming example of Columbus' superb dead reckoning navigation.

In the preceding chapters I have limited my discussion to just the technical aspects of proving that Columbus was an extremely accurate dead reckoning navigator, that his log of the 1492-1493 voyage was accurate, and that his landfall was on the island of San Salvador in the Bahamas. As you have seen, this was accomplished by re-sailing his voyage through the same

waters in a modern vessel nearly 500 years later. I have shown how the
currents which primarily affected his track are the same now as then, but
believe me that's about all that remains the same about Columbus' voyage in
the Santa Maria in 1492 and my voyages in "Gooney Bird" in 1987 and 1991.

⚓ ⚓ ⚓ ⚓ ⚓ ⚓ ⚓ ⚓

You have labored through this sometimes tedious and technical
navigational discussion so now let's look at something I hinted at in my
introduction and that is the fact that Columbus and I are kindred spirits in our
love of sailing. I can bring out this point and present a good comparison of
Columbus' 15th century voyage and my 20th century voyage with just a few
random extracts from my navigation log of the Atlantic crossing from Gomera
to landfall on San Salvador.

Like Columbus and all navigators down through time, after recording the
necessary navigational data for the day, I filled the remarks section of my log
with observations that had a bearing on the voyage. The following extracts
are taken verbatim from the remarks section of my actual log and have been
edited only to fit the space requirements of the book. Since I was reading and
following Columbus' log for each day during the voyage, my remarks contain
Columbus' observations for that day as well as mine.

As noted earlier, my reconstruction log started on 8 September (day 1)
when Columbus picked up some wind and started west, but that was a short
and relatively dull day so my first random selected extract starts the next day
(day 2):

9 September (day 2) – "Columbus rebuked his helmsmen many times for
allowing the boat to fall off to the northwest which would indicate that the
wind for him had veered around to the southeast. He mentioned earlier in the
log that he was shipping water over the bow which was slowing his progress.
He must have re-stowed ballast and stores aft because he never mentions this
again. He also doesn't mention the lousy steering by the helmsmen again so
I guess he got them straightened out.

"Unlike Columbus I didn't rebuke my autopilot for falling off course, but
I did adjust it to simulate the off course steering by the helmsmen on the Santa
Maria. My wind is still out of east-northeast about 18 knots."

13 September (day 6) – "Columbus reported that the current was against
them but without a means to measure his speed over the bottom as against the
speed through the water, there is no way he could have determined the speed

or direction of the current. Columbus like all navigators of the time estimated his speed by watching the bubbles and seaweed float by.

"Thank God I've got my good *Standard* electronic knotmeter which reads in tenths of a knot or I would never be able to duplicate his speed by watching bubbles."

14 September (day 7) – "Columbus' wind must have been dropping off and so is mine, but I still had to reduce sail to hold to the slow speed. During the night a large meteor fell into the sea near the ships and frightened the superstitious sailors but Columbus was able to calm them by convincing them it was a good omen. Columbus said the meteor hit the sea 4 or 5 leagues away but I doubt that distance. It was probably beyond the horizon and thousands of miles away but it must have been a very large meteor indeed to warrant this log entry. I see that about 110 miles north on my chart is the Great Meteor Bank, no doubt named after this event."

16 September (day 9) – "Columbus in his poetical style of writing, described the weather as 'like April in Andalusia' and then 'they met with very temperate breezes, so that it was a great delight to enjoy the mornings, and nothing was lacking save to hear nightingales.' I have temperatures in the mid 80's by day and mid 70's at night with moderate winds and a few fleecy white cumulus clouds, not unlike the weather in southern Spain in April. I even have the 'nightingales' in the form of Linda Ronstadt and Carly Simon on my stereo tapes. I'm enjoying this voyage as much as Columbus is, maybe more."

21 September (day 14) – "Columbus reported seeing a whale which he thought indicated he was near land. Columbus has a real hangup about reporting nearly everything he sees indicates he is near land. I wonder if he really believes that or is just saying so to calm the fears of the crew."

NOTE: Columbus actually had good reason to believe there were islands near him at this time in the voyage. Fifteenth century maps and written documents describing the Ocean Sea (Atlantic) and the known islands west of Europe, indicate several mythical (but firmly believed) islands along the track of Columbus' voyage. Martin Behaim's well known globe (circa 1492) shows these imaginary islands which would have been known to Columbus. A Mercator projection of the Ocean Sea portion of Behaim's globe is shown in Figure 22. Behaim's globe indicated the zero degree longitudinal meridian in this era was at Ferro (Hierro) island in the Canaries rather than at Greenwich, England where it resides today. Longitude indices are not shown on the globe

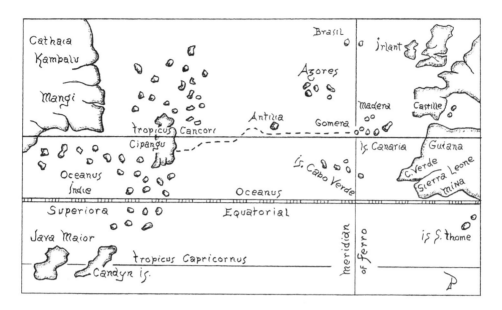

Figure 22. Mercator projection of the Ocean Sea (North Atlantic) as shown on Martin Behaim's world globe. Columbus' voyage is superimposed as a dotted line from Gomera to Cipangu.

but extrapolation of the length of a degree of longitude (as perceived by Columbus) from the circumference of the globe would place Cipangu (Japan) and the Indies at 65 degrees west longitude, about where Columbus would expect to find them. Columbus' 1492 track across the Ocean Sea (not on the original) is superimposed on the globe. Notice that Columbus' track passes just south of the mythical island of Antilia about midway in the voyage.

"I saw three pods of gray whales about 3 days ago. The pods contained between 10 to 15 whales, ranging in size from 25 to 35 feet. These are baleen whales so they feed slowly on the surface with their backs exposed, and I was able to sail right up to them before they became alarmed and suddenly they all sounded at once and disappeared.

"These are beautiful animals and I'm glad to see that most of the civilized nations in the world including Russia have stopped killing them. Only our allies, Japan and Korea continue to illegally hunt them with large ships equipped with explosive harpoons fired from large caliber guns. And sadly we are afraid to take any action in the matter because it might make these allies mad at us and then we wouldn't be able to keep thousands of American troops in their countries to protect them from their enemies and subsidize their economy."

NOTE: This remark was written in my log in 1987. The same conditions may or may not be true today.

24 September (day 17) – "For some days now Columbus has been reporting seaweed so thick that 'the sea was choked with it.' This is the area known as the Sargasso Sea and indeed is noted for its concentration of seaweed due to it being roughly near the center of the huge clockwise gyre of tropical currents in the North Atlantic. I have seen plenty of the tropical gold seaweed but it is hardly as thick as Columbus describes. Perhaps the seaweed is less now due to pollution but somehow I think Columbus is exaggerating a bit.

"What I have seen that Columbus didn't, was floating plastics which also seem to congregate in this part of the ocean. What an ugly sight! The white styrofoam cups and food containers are the most visible since they float high on the surface. But the insidious plastics are the clear plastics that float nearly submerged because the sea life mistake them for food and either eat them or become entangled in them. The turtles are especially vulnerable here since they feed on jellyfish and can easily mistake a clear plastic bag for their food. Once ingested, the plastic will not dissolve and becomes an intestinal blockage killing the turtle or other sea life."

25 September (day 18) – "Columbus sailing west all day apparently had very little winds and only made 12 nautical miles in 12 hours. This is the day that Columbus sent Toscanelli's chart over to the Pinta (they had a good day for it) and he and Pinzón (Martín Alonzo) later conferred on it when it was returned. Both agreed they were in the vicinity of islands, but they were so wrong. I have the same light winds and this has been a difficult leg as "Gooney Bird" barely has steerage to maintain the course.

The seas are smooth so I took the opportunity to do my engine maintenance. Changed the zinc in the heat exchanger, changed the #1 and #2 fuel filter elements and cleaned the #3 micronic filter. Changed the oil and oil filter and stored old oil in the bilge in empty 1 liter Coke bottles. Sanded and varnished the companionway and deck boxes and greased the winches. That ought to get me into port.

At dusk Pinzón on the Pinta saw what he thought was land to the southwest so Columbus altered course to the southwest for 12 hours during the night and I did the same. The wind must have increased because Columbus picked up to a speed of 3.8 knots making it an easier leg to sail. At dawn Columbus realized the false sighting was just a cloud below the horizon (not uncommon) and resumed a heading of west.

27 September (day 20) – "Sailing in these tropical trade winds is what it's all about. Columbus and I are both enjoying the same perfect sailing conditions, a steady 8 to 10 knot easterly following wind, smooth seas, fair skies, and moderate temperatures. I've poled out my twin genoa jibs, dropped the main and led the sheets back through blocks to the tiller so now they are self steering and will hold this course easily.

"Columbus reports the same good sailing conditions that I have but he doesn't have the autopilots and self steering devices that I have so must be bothered with a bunch of worrisome crew members to run the boat. Hooker brought in four flying fish last night and ate every one of them. That must be some kind of a record."

29 September (day 22) – "The Audubon Society would be proud of Columbus. He faithfully records every bird he sees and frequently includes detailed descriptions. This day he first reported two boobies and a frigate bird and later in the day, three boobies and a frigate bird. Since this was his first sighting of a frigate bird, he goes on to describe it quite accurately as a large scavenger bird that attacks the boobies and forces them to vomit up any recently acquired food which it promptly eats.

"Columbus also has a real hangup on nightingales, as witness his description of the weather for this day: 'The breezes were very sweet and pleasant, so that nothing was wanting save to hear the nightingale.' I guess his pleasant remarks about the nightingales will make up for his rather sordid description of the eating habits of the frigate bird. I have the same weather as Columbus. Still too much haze to get a good sighting on Polaris with my replica (the quadrant I had made), maybe tomorrow."

30 September (day 23) – "Columbus had light winds and calms and is down to 1.6 knots, my winds picked up so I dropped my twins and am jogging along on a small staysail. I finally tried my replica (quadrant). What a bummer, I give up! My best reading was sixty miles off." (see Figure 8)

2 October (day 25) – "Columbus is back up to 4.3 (knots) so I'm back on my twins, doing great, having no problem keeping up with the Old Boy. I've had two small light gray fish swimming along with me for the last three days. They swim in perfect formation with me about a foot below the surface in the shade of the hull just forward of the rudder. When I go by a large batch of seaweed, they dart off to it, I presume to feed on the small animal life in the weed, and then shortly will be back in formation. Perhaps they like the shade, or maybe they feel protected under this big fish where other predator fish

won't bother them."

11 October (day 34) – "This is the day Columbus has been waiting for and me too. I'm a bit ahead of Columbus as I picked up the light on SS (San Salvador) about 2200. My job's about over, now the paperwork starts."

Now that I look at it, that last remarks section from my log for the landfall day 11 October (12 October for us since we start our day at midnight), appears a bit short and unemotional for such a historic occasion and marking the successful completion of my voyage all the way across the Atlantic. I think I was a bit tired.

The paperwork I was referring to involved collating all my navigational data gathered on the voyage and writing my academic thesis which eventually resulted in this book. The reconstruction voyage was at times tiring and exacting work, but as you can see from this glimpse of my log and Columbus' log, there were exhilarating days at sea that more than made up for the days of toil and hardship. And in saying this I believe I can speak for both Columbus and myself.

I have shown in this chapter that my reconstructed tracks in both my 1987 and my 1991 research voyage supported San Salvador as the landfall island but there is more to the story than that. The rest of the story that will quite firmly pin down San Salvador as the true landfall island follows.

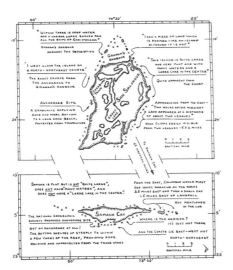

7

The True Landfall
San Salvador
vs. Samana Cay

In the preceding chapters I have established the fact that Columbus was a capable and accurate navigator, that the Atlantic track portion of his log was accurate, and that the Atlantic track from Gomera led to San Salvador (Guanahani) as the true landfall. Yet in the same breath I have reported that there are nine other widely separated islands in the Bahamas chain that vie for the claim of being the true landfall island.

The many scholars and historians who propose these other landfalls primarily base their claims on the same basic document that I used; the Las Casas summary of Columbus' navigation "diario" or log. Why the wide difference of opinion? How can this readily apparent incongruity be explained?

In Chapter 4, I touched on the reason for this wide variance of opinion as being related to the fact that these scholars primarily based their theory on the inter-island track from landfall (Guanahani) to Cuba and this is the part of Columbus' log that is the most ambiguous and devoid of definitive navigational data. In the Atlantic track portion of the log which I used, Columbus gave a definite compass heading and distance for each leg of the course, so why wasn't this same meticulous and accurate navigational data contained in the inter-island portion of the log?

The answer is probably for two perfectly logical reasons. First, Las Casas at this point deleted or severely abridged or summarized the dull navigational data to make room for the more interesting descriptions of these exotic islands and native Indians, and left just enough general directions to give some idea of the progress of the vessels through the islands.

The other reason (and most logical) could well be that Columbus was keeping his detailed navigational data on a separate portolan chart of the islands. This will be shown to be true in my later discussion of 16th century cartography. He therefore would have intentionally included only general and primarily descriptive information in his master log, since at this point the definitive navigational data was contained on the separate island chart.

But for whatever reason, the navigational data in this portion of the log is so vague, ambiguous, and nebulous that it has led many serious and intelligent scholars to study it with chimerical passion and come up with nine different widely separated landfall islands. Surely this indicates that we must look elsewhere to find the answer for the true Columbus landfall.

One of the basic precepts for solving any problem is that all matters or criteria relating to that problem must be considered in arriving at an answer. It is this basic precept that has been unmercifully violated by many scholars in their myopic historical research in which they consider only the narrow information which supports their cause and then ignore all others.

The earlier historians starting with Murdock, Humbolt, Fox, and culminating with Morison, named three criteria which an island should meet in order to qualify as the landfall island. These criteria (in chronological order only) are:

(1) The island must be at the termination of the track determined by the log from the known location of Gomera to the unknown location of the landfall on Guanahani.

(2) The island must answer the geographical and topographical description contained in the log.

(3) The island must be at the starting point of the track through the islands from the unknown location of Guanahani to the known location of the Ragged Islands and Cuba (the inter-island track).

Early on in my research of the Columbus voyage I realized that these three criteria were incomplete and did not consider other valuable historical information that was available in extant historical documents. Accordingly I prepared an eclectic essay "Re-thinking the Landfall Problem" in which I proposed that these three criteria should be expanded to five in order to adequately cover the subject and thus with accuracy determine the true landfall. This essay was presented in a lecture (by proxy: Dr. J. H. Fitzgerald) to the "Society for the History of Discoveries" in 1992 at their annual meeting in Miami. These two additional and vital determining criteria are:

(4) Be the island Ponce de León identified as "Guanahani" in the navigational log of his 1513 discovery voyage.

(5) Be the island identified as "Guanahani" in early 16th century cartography made from contemporary and unbiased sources.

When I was formulating the expansion of the criteria from three to five,

I considered a sixth which would have been the archaeological evidence. I had to rule this criterion out because all archaeological finds to date only establish the fact that there was both a Taino Indian and a Spanish presence in the islands in the late 15th and early 16th century. We know that already, so even though it gives us interesting historical information, it doesn't tell us a thing that will help solve the problem of the landfall island. For this reason I have limited the criteria to the five listed as I believe that will now give us the full and complete information to arrive at the true answer.

Chapters 5 & 6 of this book firmly establishes San Salvador as satisfying the first criteria of being at the termination of the track from Gomera to landfall on Guanahani. Now let's examine this first criterion and the other four criteria and see how San Salvador stands up to the other contenders.

And in this respect I find that I must narrow the nine proposed landfall islands down to just the two islands in the central Bahamas that are supported by the most viable and consummated research by reputable and recognized authorities in this discipline. I hasten to add that I do this with some temerity since I am sure this is going to offend a number of my respected colleagues in this discipline who feel very strongly that they are the only ones who have interpreted Columbus' log correctly to substantiate their particular island.

Currently the only two islands that merit our attention are San Salvador, proposed and substantiated by Samuel Eliot Morison in the *Admiral of the Ocean Sea* in 1942, and Samana Cay proposed and substantiated by Joseph Judge in the *National Geographic* magazine in 1986. At this point I will discuss how each of these two islands stand up to the five essential criteria I have listed:

Criterion (1) - The island must be at the termination of the Atlantic track from Gomera:

San Salvador is the winner here but only because of my empirical reconstruction of the track (Chapters 5 & 6). I have shown that McElroy's plotted track (for Morison) was based on artificial and arbitrary control factors that forced the track to go where he desired. Some other recent computer generated Atlantic tracks have in like manner been flawed by use of the same poorly substantiated or speculative control factors. My empirical reconstruction overcomes these flawed control factors and firmly backs up Morison in this criterion by naming (and proving) San Salvador as the landfall island.

Luis Marden supported Samana Cay for the National Geographic Society by a computer generated plot of the Atlantic track which also used suspect or erroneous control factors programmed into his computer. Marden's control factor for Columbus' estimate of speed and so distance was based on

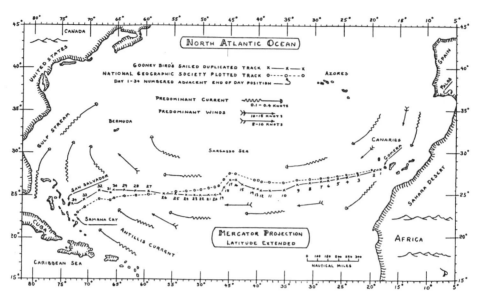

Figure 23. Chart showing the National Geographic Society plotted track and the "Gooney Bird" sailed and reconstructed track from Gomera to landfall.

a postulated length of the Spanish league (which he assumes Columbus was using) of 2.82 nautical miles to the league that he found in a 16th century English document. Then using that 2.82 nautical mile factor as applied to Columbus' reporting of the distance covered in his log, he has his plotted track end exactly at Samana Cay. (see Figure 23)

Marden's application of (non-existent) leeway to his computations would have introduced an error in his track, but since I do not know how he programmed this into his computer I cannot say to what degree this would have affected the track. However, I can point out two very positive things wrong with Marden's plotted track. The first is that Columbus used the shorter Mediterranean factor of 2.67 nautical miles to the league for his estimate of speed and distance rather than the longer Spanish factor, which I have proved conclusively in the preceding chapters. The second is Marden's plot is based on the flawed magnetic variation of Van Bemmelen and the inaccurate and insufficient ocean currrent data from the pilot charts. Marden is not alone here as all recent plotting of the Atlantic track by theoretical navigators with their computers have used these same flawed and inappropriate control factors.

In the paper on my 1987 reconstruction of the Columbus Atlantic track I had a detailed analysis of the National Geographic Society's plotted track and showed how (and why) the two tracks differed. Figure 23 is the chart from my 1987 paper and graphically shows the difference between the National Geographic Society's flawed track to Samana Cay and my empirical reconstructed track to San Salvador. You will recall that my 1991 track shown in Chapter 6 supports this earlier finding by deviating only slightly from the 1987 track from Gomera to San Salvador.

Criterion (2) - The island must conform to the geographical description of Guanahani as contained in Columbus' log:

Here once again San Salvador is clearly the winner. But why? In my 1987 and 1991 reconstruction voyages I approached both San Salvador and Samana Cay from the east and then conducted a detailed physical examination to see how each island would answer Columbus' description of his landfall island. (I might add that I am the only one of the many scholars involved who has done this.)

Columbus devoted more time (222 lines in his log) to describing the geographical features of Guanahani (his landfall) than he did to any of the subsequent islands he was to discover. His description of the geography and topography with emphasis on the shoreline is in minute detail. He stated it was fairly large, level and fertile, with many waters (ponds), a large lake or lagoon in the center, with several settlements of many people, infers a good anchorage on the west side, and states he followed the coastline in a north-northeast direction ending (at the north end) in a large harbor surrounded by reefs with a peninsula on one side. San Salvador has all of the features as described while Samana Cay and the other contestants have virtually none.

Efforts by the advocates of Samana Cay and the other islands to explain away the disparity between the geographical features described in the log and their island becomes a tortured and unreal mental exercise in making a large island out of a small one, or producing ponds, lagoons, and harbors where none exist, or even making one island out of an archipelago of several, so that it becomes almost ludicrous.

Take a good close look at the graphic presentation with its annotated notes shown in Figure 24 and it will show better than words how Columbus' description fits San Salvador very closely and Samana Cay not at all.

Even the Indians in their orthographic method of naming the islands of Guanahani and Samana provided strong evidence that San Salvador was the landfall island. The Taino Indians invariably based the name of an island on some prominent geographical feature of the island or on its relative position within the Lucayan (Bahamas) chain of islands. Julian Granberry, who is the foremost authority on the Arawak language (the language of the Taino Indians), has shown that the etymological meaning of "Guanahani" was

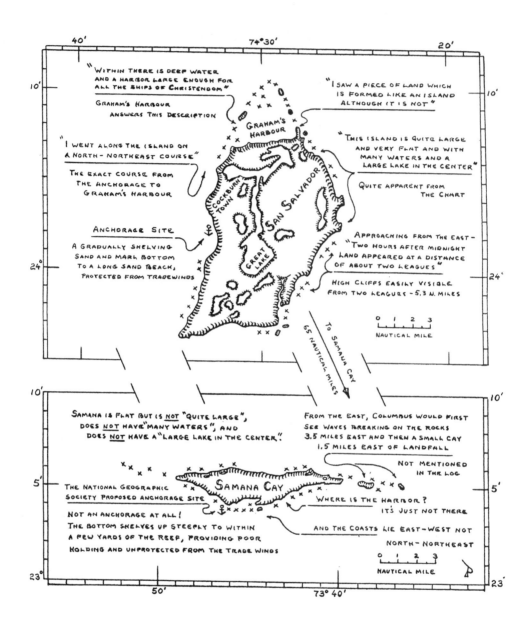

Figure 24. A chart comparing geographical features of San Salvador and Samana Cay as related to Columbus' description of the landfall island. The annotated descriptive notes on the chart are taken directly from Columbus' log.

"Small Upper Waters Land", and "Samana" means "Small Unforested Land." Let's analyze each of these names and relate them to the geographical description in Columbus' log.

The key words in the Indian's geographical description of Guanahani is "Small", "Upper", and "Waters". The descriptive word "Small" derives from the fact that it is the smallest of the three other neighboring islands in the group which has the term "Upper" in their name (Bahama I., Andros I., and Crooked-Acklins I.). And of course the word "Waters" in the name means it has ample fresh water ponds. All of this fits the island of San Salvador!

The key words in the Indian's description of Samana are "Small", and "Unforested." The word "Small" in this instance cannot be related to any other island since this is the only "Unforested" island named. But the fact that it is "Unforested" clearly means that it is a small arid island incapable of supporting the several Indian settlements reported by Columbus. Contrast this with what Columbus said about Guanahani after his landing. Columbus reported (13 October) that on Guanahani "the trees are very green and there is much water," then later reported "there are the loveliest group of trees that I have ever seen, all green and with leaves like those of Castile in the months of April and May, and much water." How can Samana (Samana Cay) be the island of Guanahani if it was arid and unforested in Columbus' time as it is today?

I'm not sure where the National Geographic Society obtained their geography consultants for the Columbus landfall article but they should have gone to Professor Neil Sealey of the College of the Bahamas in Nassau. Neil Sealey is recognized as an authority on diagnostic research pertaining to the geographical development of the Bahamas island chain from the Pleistocene period to the present. Sealey presented a scholarly and thoroughly documented thesis on the geography involved in the landfall controversy (*Terrae Incognitae* and *Caribbean Geography*) which shows clearly that the National Geographic Society is poorly informed on the geography of the islands. This study was centered on the three landfall contenders: San Salvador, Samana Cay, and Grand Turk Island. In his analysis of the 1492 geographical features of these islands, compared to the description by Columbus (and Oviedo), Sealey quite firmly shows that San Salvador meets the description far ahead of the others.

I then continued my physical examination and comparison of both San Salvador and Samana Cay. After approaching San Salvador from the east and determining that it answered Columbus' description, I later sailed overnight in a south-southeasterly direction to Samana Cay and approached it from the east as Columbus would have done to see how it would answer Columbus' description in the log. I first ran into several exposed rocks and small islands three and a half nautical miles offshore at about the point that Columbus says he first sighted land. Columbus doesn't mention this fact even though as a prudent navigator he would certainly have noted this hazard to navigation in his log.

I must pause here and address the fact that some scholars in desperately trying to eliminate (or explain) unreported hazards to the east of their proposed islands cite the fact that Oviedo, a Spanish historian and contemporary of Columbus, states that Columbus approached Guanahani from the north in direct contradiction to Columbus' reports in his log. (Although some linquists have interpreted Oviedo as "to " the north rather than "from" the north.) In this instance we must consider that Oviedo based this remark on testimony given well after the event and from crew members who were trying to establish the fact that Martín Alonzo Pinzón was the real discoverer of the islands when he urged Columbus to sail to the southwest (which Columbus ignored) late in the voyage. Oviedo's remark here falls in the same category as his spurious statement in the same document that the islands that Columbus discovered were really found by a Visigoth navigator from Spain centuries before Columbus. These facts clearly discredit Oviedo's after the fact (and biased) testimony, so it should be ignored and the testimony of the log should prevail.

After approaching Samana Cay from the east (as Columbus' log shows) I carefully circled the entire cay to see if it would answer Columbus' description. It not only didn't conform to Columbus' geographical description, but I could not find Columbus' anchorage or the "great harbor" he found on the north end, and the reason is they simply do not exist on Samana Cay.

The National Geographic Society has clearly failed to show that Samana Cay even comes close to the geographical description of the landfall so let's move on to the third criterion.

Criterion (3) - The island must be at the starting point of the inter-island track from Guanahani to Cuba.

This is the weakest and least reliable criteria of the five named, which is amply demonstrated by the fact that it is the primary reason for nine different and widely separated landfall islands appearing on the scene. Any reader who thinks I am alone in this assessment should read David Henige's excellent book on the subject, *In Search of Columbus*. However, we must consider this criterion in some detail since both Morison and the National Geographic Society use an analysis and a plot of this track to support their respective landfalls. To give the reader a feel for this meandering and complicated track, I have shown the Morison track from San Salvador and the National Geographic Society track from Samana Cay in Figure 25.

It is beyond the scope of this narrative to give a detailed description of

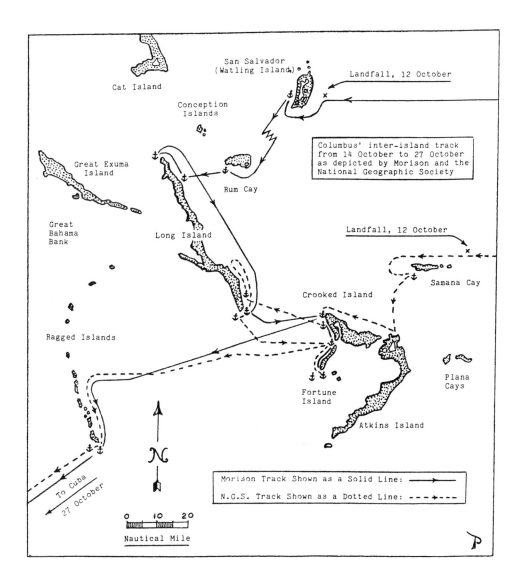

Figure 25. A scaled chart to show the wide difference between the inter-island track proposed by Samuel Eliot Morison and the track proposed by the National Geographic Society. The wide differnce in these two tracks gives a graphic presentation and argument to show that Columbus' log of his meandering track through the islands cannot be used with any degree of confidence to identify the landfall island.

the theoretical tracks of either Morison or the National Geographic Society so I will only point out how widely they differ and cover the weak and controversial points in each track.

Samuel Eliot Morison's inter-island track was first shown in his voluminous and superbly documented book *Admiral of the Ocean Sea* published in 1942. Morison based his track (and so states in his writings) on the previous research of J. B. Murdock (see bibliography). This is the best and most logical of all of the many proposed tracks, but because it is based on such misleading and sometimes non-existing navigational data, it has its weak points and even obvious faults. In fact we will find that the National Geographic Society bases much of their argument for Samana Cay in a negative attack on Morison rather than a positive approach to support their own theory.

The weak points in the Morison track have recently been clarified and supported by the research of a number of my colleagues in the Society for the History of Discoveries.

Dr. Donald Gerace has been the Chief Executive Officer for the Bahamian Field Station of the Universities of the Finger Lakes for many years. In this capacity he has made a detailed academic and field study of the geological and geographical nature of the islands from the Columbian historical period to date. His several published and unpublished essays on the geological and geographical formation of the islands confirms the fact that Columbus' description of Guanahani fits San Salvador far better than any other island. Dr. Gerace's findings in this instance are in complete agreement with the independent findings of Neil Sealey reported earlier.

Dr. Gerace in a controlled field experiment presented irrefutable evidence that Columbus would be able to row his small boats (as indicated in the log) from his anchorage on the western shore of San Salvador to the large harbor (Graham's Harbor) at the north end of the island. This is a point that the National Geographic Society (with an irrelevant comment from Tim Severin) uses in an attempt to rule out the larger San Salvador in favor of the smaller Samana Cay. Dr. Gerace is a trained and experienced scholar who has been associated with the subject for many years, so why doesn't anyone listen to him?

James E. Kelley Jr. has presented a number of well documented arguments that support the Morison theory and one of his best is a recent essay in *Terrae Incognitae* in which he documents the postulated geographical size and Indian population of Guanahani as indicated in Columbus' log. In this study Kelley presented evidence to show that San Salvador could easily support the existence of the several villages and fairly large population of

Indians reported by Columbus while the small, arid ("unforested") and historically unpopulated Samana Cay would be unable to do so.

As stated earlier, the Morison track does have its weakpoints but these are primarily confined to difficulty in defining Columbus' exact anchorages rather than the general path through the islands. William Dunwoody and William Keegan in independent research have provided minor revisions to the Morison track that makes it a more viable solution. Keegan's expertise in the Bahamas has been primarily in the disciplines of archaeology and anthropology but in 1982 he initiated a program together with Steven Mitchell, a geologist from California State University, to try and disprove the then dominant Morison theory. After working on this project for nearly a decade, Keegan in his recent book has this to say about Morison's designation of San Salvador as the landfall: "After seven years of trying to prove otherwise, I am now convinced that San Salvador Island is the island the Lucayans called Guanahani." Would that we had more astute scholars like Keegan who, when confronted with overwhelming documented evidence, would have the courage to change their position without fear of losing face.

One of the primary arguments that the National Geographic Society put forward for Samana Cay concerns the "many islands" that Columbus claimed he could see shortly after leaving Guanahani. Their argument here is that the "many islands" can be seen from the vicinity of Samana Cay and not San Salvador. Columbus could not possibly have optically seen "many islands" after leaving either Samana Cay or San Salvador as any navigator with experience sailing in the islands will tell you.

The Indian guides had told Columbus there were "many islands" just over the horizon, and he knew from his reading of Marco Polo that the Indies (where he thought he was) consisted of "many islands." At this exciting time is he going to put into the log for the eyes of Ferdinand and Isabela that he is sailing off for islands that he can't see but the Indians assured him are there? Of course not! He would, with complete faith, say he saw them because he knew his positive statement would be vindicated.

And what does Columbus really mean when he says he "saw" these many islands? My English-Spanish dictionary gives several meanings for the verb "to see" (vide), one of which is to "comprehend" or "be aware of" (as I "see" what you mean). This different definition (or translation) of "saw" (vide) is supported by the very next sentence in which Columbus states the Indians; "told me (or made him "aware of") by signs that they (islands) were so many that they were numberless." But regardless, let's concede the narrow optical definition of "vide" and take a look at the National Geographic Society argument on this point.

The National Geographic Society enlisted the aid of the Control Data Corporation to come up with a computer study that would prove their point about the "many islands" that can be seen from Samana Cay. This study is on page 588 and 589 of the November 1986 issue of the *National Geographic* magazine. The computer study is based upon the mathematical theoretical sighting range or the theoretical circle of visibility. This theoretical sighting range is based upon a mathematical projection of a viewer's line of sight passing just inches over the curvature of the earth's surface at the horizon and picking up the top few inches of the highest elevation on an island in unlimited visibility. Far more than the top few inches of an island must be above the horizon for the naked eye to see it, and unlimited visibility never exists in the Bahamas because of the heavy sea haze. For this reason, the theoretical sighting range is completely irrelevant in this instance, yet the National Geographic Society uses it as one of their strongest points for supporting Samana Cay.

The Control Data Corporation did just what it had been instructed to do with their computer study and (I quote from page 589) "located 117 islands in the group." (Really now! - 117 islands?) Then, and again I quote: "Artist William H. Bond has translated the computer's circles of visibility into a landscape that a sailor would see." The artist quite apparently took those unrealistic pinpoints on the computer readout and pictured them as volcanic looking peaks towering above the horizon and the *National Geographic* magazine has the audacity to tell the reader that is what Columbus saw when departing Samana Cay!

As I stated earlier, this article naming Samana Cay as the landfall island is a contrived and strained effort that is not up to the usual high standard of excellence that we have come to expect from the *National Geographic* magazine.

Although the meandering and uncertain inter-island track is only a weak corroborating factor, it can be seen that on this criterion San Salvador is well ahead of Samana Cay.

Criterion (4) - The Ponce de León voyage track which identifies and locates Guanahani in the central Bahamas:

Ponce de León in his 1513 discovery voyage from Puerto Rico to the shores of Florida landed on an island in the Bahamas which his Indian guides told him was Guanahani, the landfall of Columbus. Ponce de León left a navigator's log (contained in Antonio de Herrera's *Historia*) giving compass courses, distances, descriptions of landfalls, Indian names of islands, even latitudes, so it provides a perfect secondary and unbiased document to locate and identify the present day island that was the Guanahani of Columbus' landfall.

For this reason I elected to undertake a research voyage in "Gooney Bird" and faithfully followed Ponce de León's log as I had done Columbus' log. My goal was to determine which island in the Bahamas was Guanahani, then to locate just exactly where he landed on the shores of Florida. This research voyage was performed in 1990, following which I wrote an academic paper which was published in the October, 1992 issue of the *Florida Historical Quarterly.* This was followed by a more comprehensive book on the voyages of Ponce de León titled *Ponce de León and the Discovery of Florida,* published in September 1993. The navigational data presented here will be taken from the Bahamas segment of the 1992 article and the 1993 book

Ponce de León was an aristocrat and a conquistador and no seaman or navigator so the navigational data in the log is from his pilot Antón de Alaminos. Alaminos came over with Columbus (probably on the second voyage) as a young apprentice seaman and stayed in the islands to become one of the most experienced and sought after pilots of the Indies. As an up from the ranks Spanish pilot, Alaminos (like Columbus) would have navigated by dead reckoning on a portolan chart, but because he gave the latitudes of some of the islands, there are those who mistakenly assume (without foundation) that he used celestial observations to obtain those latitudes.

Some scholars question the validity of using the navigational data in Herrera's account of the Ponce de León voyage because it is a summary of the log rather than a direct copy of the original holograph log. Herrera summarized and abridged Ponce de León's log in the same manner that Las Casas summarized and abridged Columbus' log. Both were done from the original holograph document or a scribe's copy.

Unfortunately Herrera added numerous comments that were based on knowledge obtained long after 1513, and were not contained in the original log. This has led some scholars to believe that Herrera authored the entire account and that the navigational data are his and not extracted from the original log. However, these additions by Herrera are easily identified, and when they are removed, the original log entries of compass headings, times, distances, descriptions of landfalls, latitudes, identification of known islands with Indian names, sea conditions, and weather—all of which are elements of a navigator's log—come through with clarity. Why should they lose their value just because they come to us summarized by a second person?

Ponce de León departed Point Aguada on the western shore of Puerto Rico and sailed for about four days on a heading of northwest, a quarter by north and landed on an island which he called "El Viejo" on the banks of

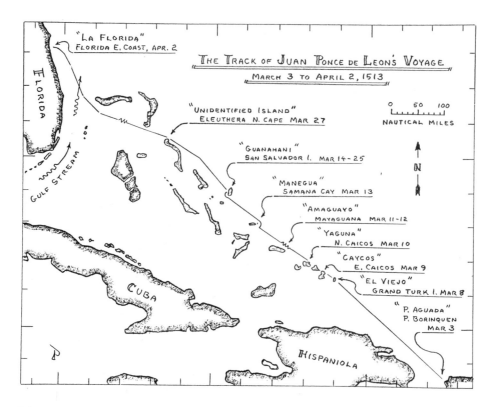

Figure 26. The track of Ponce de León showing the sequence of islands in the Bahamas encountered before arriving at San Salvador (Guanahani).

"Babueca." In re-sailing this course I found that "El Viejo" could easily be identified as Grand Turk island. The Ponce de León track from Puerto Rico through the Bahamas to Florida is shown in Figure 26.

The log gives the latitude of "El Viejo" as 22 degrees, 30 minutes, while the actual latitude of Grand Turk is 21 degrees, 25 minutes (from the anchorage on the bank south). This placement of the latitude a little over one degree too far north will be reflected to some degree in all later latitudes in the log. The reason for this is quite obvious as Alaminos started his dead reckoning from Point Aguada with a northerly error on his chart. This is quite understandable since all early sixteenth century charts and rutters (navigator's guide) consistently showed known landmarks in the New World as several degrees too far north (see my remarks in Chapter 6).

From Grand Turk the track passed the islands of "Caycos" (E. Caicos), "Yaguna" (N. Caicos), "Amaguayo" (Mayaguana), "Manegua" (Samana Cay), and finally arrived at "Guanahani" (San Salvador). Identification of these islands on the Ponce de León track quite effectively rules out five of the nine contenders south of Guanahani (San Salvador). This track which was easily followed from the log is shown in Figure 26.

While I have gone though this track rapidly here, it is fully documented and proved in my technical papers and book previously mentioned. Ponce de León's track through the islands can also be visualized by referring to the Jean Rotz chart in Figure 27 which carries the annotations of the principal islands he encountered.

It is the portion of my reconstruction of the Ponce de León track as it approaches and arrives at Samana Cay and then San Salvador in which we are most interested, and I can do no better than quote from my 1993 book to give an accurate description of this part of the track:

"From Mayaguana they sailed to an island they called 'Manegua' which they apparently passed by without stopping and reported it lies at 24 degrees, 30 minutes latitude. As the chart shows (Figure 26), this is clearly Samana Cay whose latitude is 23 degrees, 03 minutes, once again showing that Alaminos by his dead reckoning is retaining his original northerly error.

"This is the small, barren, and uninhabited cay which the National Geographic Society has named as 'Guanahani' the landfall island of Columbus. However Ponce de León does not arrive at Guanahani until the next day and about 65 miles farther (an overnight sail) along the northwesterly course. Who is right here? Ponce de León says Samana Cay is 'Manegua' (and early 16th century cartography agrees) but the National Geographic Society says it's 'Guanahani'. I'll opt for Ponce de León since he had two Indian guides with him who certainly could correctly identify both 'Manegua' and 'Guanahani.' The National Geographic Society, without benefit of Indian guides, was forced to come up with a tortured and contrived reconstruction of a portion of Columbus' navigational log (the inter-island track) to justify naming Samana Cay as Guanahani.

"Ponce de León passed by Samana Cay without anchoring, and I know why. A suitable and safe anchorage just doesn't exist on Samana Cay for vessels the size and draft of Ponce de León's (and Columbus') caravels. In 1987 when I made an analytical and field study of Columbus' 1492 discovery voyage, I approached Samana Cay from the east in 'Gooney Bird' and circled the entire cay but could not find Columbus' anchorage or the 'great Harbor' he found on the north end, and the reason is they simply do not exist on Samana Cay.

"I made one more attempt to find an anchorage site during this voyage in 1990, watching my depthometer and poking into shore within a few hundred feet of the reefs that surround the cay, and again could not find a shelf suitable or safe for either Columbus or Ponce de León to anchor their caravels.

Yet the theoretical navigators of the National Geographic Society have shown on their chart of Samana Cay an anchorage where an anchorage does not exist!

"…. We now rejoin Ponce de León sailing northwesterly from Manegua (Samana Cay) seeking Guanahani where he will hop off in the search for his island of Beniny. The log at this point reads, '…at the 14th they came to Guanahani, which lies in 25 degrees, 40 minutes (latitude), where they trimmed up one ship in order to cross the windward sea of those islands of the Lucayans.' He then identified the island as the one that 'Christoval Colon' (Columbus) discovered in 1492.

"Alaminos reports the latitude of Guanahani as 25 degrees, 40 minutes, when it is actually 24 degrees, zero minutes, once more showing that Alaminos was determining his latitudes from his dead reckoning chart and thus carrying his original northerly error through the entire voyage. It is interesting to note that later in the voyage Alaminos reports that Key West and the adjacent keys lie at 26 degrees, 15 minutes, while the keys actually lie at 24 degrees, 35 minutes, so his northerly error at that known point was one degree, 40 minutes, about the midpoint or average of his northerly errors. Then if we take that one degree, 40 minute average northerly error and subtract it from his report of Guanahani lying at 25 degrees, 40 minutes, the result would be a latitude of 24 degrees, right through the middle of San Salvador!

"In both my 1987 and my 1991 re-sailing and reconstruction of Columbus' discovery voyage, I ended up at San Salvador to pinpoint it as Guanahani, the island of Columbus' landfall. Now with the identification of San Salvador as Guanahani from both Ponce de León's log and Columbus' log, we have what in navigation parlance is referred to as a positive fix (when two tracks from independent sources cross each other). So Ponce de León has made his first significant discovery in this voyage by naming the Bahamas island of San Salvador as Columbus' landfall in the New World."

The independent and unbiased identification of San Salvador as Columbus' landfall island of Guanahani by the Ponce de León log provides an overwhelmingly strong determining factor that has been overlooked or ignored by most historians in this discipline. The reader can easily see that this added criterion supplies overpowering evidence to refute the National Geographic Society's claim that Samana Cay (and others as well) is the landfall of Columbus. But there is more!

Criterion (5) - The evidence supplied by early 16th century cartography:

I cannot understand the reluctance of historians to accept early 16th century maps and charts as contributing valuable information to identify the landfall island of Columbus. Most detractors of this important criterion cite the fact that early charts and maps of the Bahamas contain distortion, inconsistencies, and obvious errors. All of this is true, but that is no reason to throw the baby out with the bathwater. Through a careful study of the many available maps can be found a thread of truth that shines through the inconsistencies to show how the early explorers and cartographers recorded the relative positions of the key islands of the Bahamas accurately enough for us to identify Guanahani and its related islands.

My colleagues in the Society for the History of Discoveries have done some excellent research in this area that has not received just recognition. Donald L. McGuirk Jr. has produced a number of published and unpublished essays that point to San Salvador as the landfall island. The latest and best published paper on this subject is the brilliant essay by Kim Dian Gainer in the 1988 issue of *Terrae Incognitae*. Gainer gives a comprehensive analysis of all the significant early charts beginning with the Juan de la Cosa map of the New World (circa 1500) through the later Spanish, Portuguese, Italian, Dutch, and English charts to the middle of the 17th century. This well documented thesis shows clearly that even though Guanahani and its related islands change spelling and sometimes migrate around the central Bahamas, a clear pattern emerges that places the landfall (Guanahani) on San Salvador south of Cat Island and north of Samana Cay.

Here we should return to my Ponce de León northwesterly track (Figure 26) from Mayaguana to Samana Cay (Manegua) to San Salvador (Guanahani) and see if this sequence of islands from Ponce de León's log is borne out by 16th century cartography. The Jean Rotz map (1542) in Figure 27 shows how Ponce de León's log is verified by a map which was compiled from several other reliable sources about three decades after the voyage. But there are other maps both before and after the Rotz map that show Guanahani and its neighboring islands north and south that will allow us to pinpoint the location of San Salvador as Guanahani the landfall island.

The editors of "A Columbus Casebook", published by the *National Geographic* magazine (November, 1986), admit that Ponce de León reached Manegua prior to stopping at Guanahani. Then to explain away this problem, boldly (and without any foundation) announced that Manegua is not Samana Cay but is in fact Mayaguana. Really now? Let's look at what 16th century cartography tells us about the identification and location of Manegua, Mayaguana, and Guanahani and we will quickly see that the "experts" who wrote "A Columbus Casebook" have made a completely unfounded and erroneous statement in order to extricate themselves from the untenable position in which Ponce de León's log has placed them.

To pin down the location of Guanahani in the Bahamas chain of islands

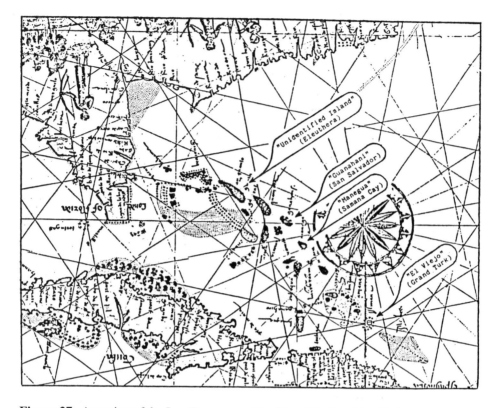

Figure 27. A portion of the Jean Rotz map of the New World, with added notations of the pertinent islands reported in Ponce de León's log.

it is necessary to identify and locate the several prominent islands immediately north and south of Guanahani. Following is a study of five of the most authoritative early 16th century maps and two early 17th century maps (based on 16th century sources) with an analysis of the relationship of the known islands north and south of Guanahani to substantiate its location. The spelling of each island varies as it is taken from the individual map and the modern name of each island is shown in parenthesis.

The map of the New World by Juan de la Cosa (circa 1500):

Both the date and the authorship of this map (Figure 28) is uncertain, but it is recognized as being an early Portolan type chart and based on first hand knowledge. None of Columbus' holograph maps (or charts) of the islands have survived but there are a number of extant maps that lay claim to being a copy of one of Columbus' original maps of the Indies. Prominent among these are the Turkish Piri Reis map of 1513 and the Spanish Juan de la Cosa map of 1500. A comprehensive study of the Piri Reis map by Gregory

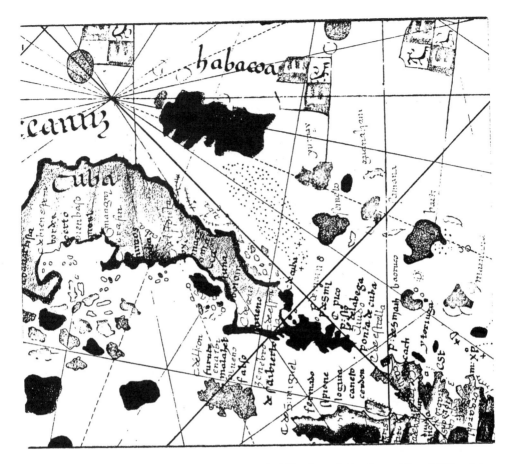

Figure 28. Detail from the map of the New World by Juan de La Cosa. Circa 1500 or later.

McIntosh indicates that this map can indeed be traced to Columbus but it suffers for navigational accuracy because it was developed from one of Columbus' earliest maps (well before the 1513 date). The map thus contains Columbus' intentional distortion of geography of the area to try and show that he had reached Cipangu and the Mainland of China.

A similar detailed study of the Juan de la Cosa map by Donald McGuirk indicates that it is derived from one of Columbus' later maps and so is a more reliable source for navigational data. There are several things that indicate this map was derived from Columbus' original chart of the islands. First and foremost is the fact that Guanahani (the landfall island) is shown in the extreme northeastern part of the Bahamas. After leaving Guanahani, Columbus traveled in a general southwesterly direction so he would have shown Guanahani on his chart as depicted. Another fact is that "Someto" (Columbus' Saometo) is shown southwest of Guanahani where it would have appeared on

Columbus' chart. This map does not point to any particular island in the Bahamas in a definitive manner as those to follow, but a significant fact is that "Samana" is shown as a separate island just south of "Guanahani."

It should be noted that this is a small detail of a much larger world map. As such the depiction of the islands is much simplified and abbreviated from the more detailed and accurate navigator's chart of the area from which this part was derived. Unfortunately none of these highly perishable navigator's charts (including Columbus') of this restricted area made their way into the archives of Europe. Thus it must be realized that this and the maps to follow do not have the accuracy required for navigation of the area, but nevertheless even in their simplified form will give us enough reliable navigational data to determine the true landfall of Columbus.

The map of the New World from the portolan atlas of Vesconti de Maggiolo (1511):

This is one of the first maps that definitely points to San Salvador by showing "Guanima" (Cat Island) immediately north of "Guanahani" (San Salvador). Then "Zamena" (Samana Cay) is shown immediately south in a reasonably close conformance to their actual positions.

The anonymous "Turin" world map (1523):

By the period of this map the chain of islands both north and south is beginning to fill in and the compass bearings between islands is improving. At the extreme north (of our group) is "Ziguateo" (Eleuthera), then in a southeasterly direction comes "Guanima" (Cat Island), "Gunahani" (San Salvador), "Manigua" (Samana Cay), followed by "Mayaguana" (Mayaguana). This is one of the first of the early maps where the island of "Samana" has changed to "Manigua"/"Manegua". The island reverts to its original "Samana" name after the Ponce de León period around 1530-1540.

The world map of Diego Ribero (1527):

Here again from the north we find; "Cigateo" (Eleuthera), "Guanima" (Cat Island), "Guanahan" (San Salvador), "Manigua" (Samana Cay), then "Mayaguano" (Mayaguana). This follows the exact sequence of the islands named and once again the distance and compass bearings between islands is improving. Notice that the last two well recognized and accepted maps which fall in the Ponce de León era, both list "Manegua" and "Mayaguana" as two separate islands yet the National Geographic Society says they are one and the same. I almost hesitate to say (with tongue in cheek), that perhaps the editors of the *National Geographic* magazine need to take a course in geography.

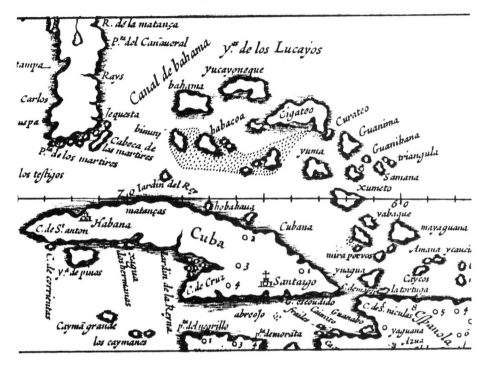

Figure 29. Detail from Juan Lopez de Velasco's map of the New World, in Antonio de Herrera y Tordesillas' *Novus Orbi*s, published in Amsterdam (1622).

The map from Jean Rotz *Boke of Idrography* (1542):

This map (shown earlier in Figure 27) made from Portuguese, Spanish, French, and English sources, was prepared after years of study in the University of Paris and other leading European universities and after participation in several voyages to the New World. Jean Rotz in his *Boke of Idrography* also gave a treatise on magnetic variation in the early 16th century which was used in my study of magnetic variation in Chapter 4. The track of Ponce de León along the annotated islands can be easily correlated with his track shown in Figures 26 & 27. This firm correlation of the Ponce de León log with early 16th century cartography lends weight, in fact quite firmly establishes, the log as a primary determining factor in naming the landfall island. Here once again Guanahani is firmly established as San Salvador with Cat Island Guanima) just to the northwest and Samana Cay (Manegua) to the southeast.

The map of Juan Lopez de Velasco (1622):

This map (Figure 29) although published in the early 17th century follows closely earlier 16th century Spanish maps. Again Guanihana is shown

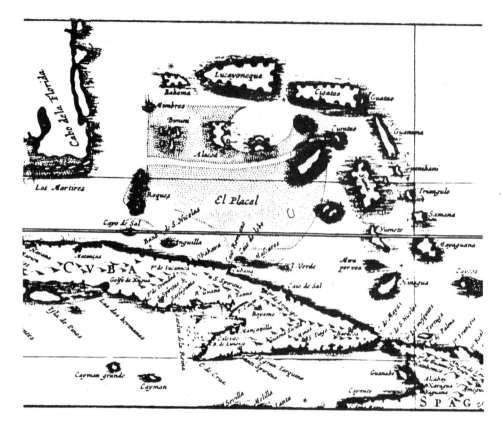

Figure 30. Detail from Joannes de Laet's map of the New World, published in *Nieuvve Wereldt Ofte Beschrijvinghe van West-Indien*, Leyden (1625).

in the position of San Salvador with Guanima (Cat Island) shown correctly just to the northwest and Samana (Samana Cay) and Mayaguana (Mayaguana) to the southeast. About this period, the non-existing small Triangula islands appeared on maps in the general area of Guanahani (Guanihana), only to disappear from the scene a few decades later.

The map of Joannes de Laet (1625):

This Dutch map (Figure 30) published in Leyden perpetuates and improves on the Spanish tradition with regard to the identification and positioning of Guanahani. The Dutch were more precise than the Spanish in showing the islands of the Bahamas in their correct relationship to each other in both compass bearings and distances. Here we see Guanahani (correctly spelled) easily identified as San Salvador because of its position in relation to seven of its neighboring Bahamas islands in a remarkably accurate depiction of marine geography for the time period. (see Figure 30)

Cat Island (Guanima) is shown correctly just northwest of San Salvador (Guanahani) and Eleuthera (Cigateo) is shown farther in a northwesterly direction. Then on the map moving southwest from Guanahani (the direction Columbus sailed) we find Rum Cay (unnamed), then farther west (in the direction Columbus sailed) is Long Island (Yuma). From there in a south-southeasterly direction (approximating the direction Columbus sailed) is the Crooked-Atkins Island archipelago (Columbus' Saometo, here called Yumeto). Note the path I have just followed from Guanahani follows the path through the islands advocated by Morison and the compass headings sailed agree with those in the log. (see Figure 25).

Now moving in a southeasterly direction from Guanahani (San Salvador) we find the non-existent Triangulo (later to be removed from maps) followed by Samana (Samana Cay) then Mayaguana (Mayaguana) in the exact order and direction that these islands exist in the Bahamas. Here once again the island of Guanahani is positively identified as San Salvador with Cat Island correctly positioned just to the northwest and Samana Cay shown correctly in a southeasterly direction.

Does this Dutch map have its faults and distortions? Of course it does! The shorelines have the usual unreal scallops that are common to European maps of this era. Some small islands are omitted while the island of Triangulo that doesn't exist is included. And the exact shape and size of the islands leaves something to be desired. But remember that this is a detail of a much larger world map not intended for navigation. Also this is an area of little interest, so the cartographer was primarily interested in showing the correct Indian name and the correct geographical position in the overall chain of islands. And that is all we are interested in at the moment, so this map together with the other maps shown, provides a viable and accurate source for identifying the landfall island.

There are more early maps that show this same pattern but this is enough to firmly establish the fact that the present day San Salvador is in fact the Guanahani of Columbus' landfall. And further, that the present day Samana Cay is in fact the early Samana or Manegua, an island separate from Guanahani and located some distance to the south-southeast of it. Also firmly established is the fact that the early Manegua (of the Ponce de León log) is the present day Samana Cay and not Mayaguana as so boldly asserted by the National Geographic Society in "A Columbus Casebook."

And these early maps are not the only 16th century documents to position Guanahani on the island of San Salvador. The rutter or *derrotero* (navigator's guide) of Alonzo de Chávez (circa 1530) gives a verbal picture of the islands in the Bahamas by reporting their relative compass bearings and distances from each other. James Kelly has produced an excellent analysis of this rutter (see bibliography) which resolves some of the minor inconsistencies and transcription errors inherent in all these early documents. Chávez's rutter places Guanahani in the central Bahamas with the separate islands of Samana (Samana Cay), Mayaguana, (Mayaguana), and Caycos (Caicos and Turks islands) to the south and Guanima (Cat Island), and Cigateo (Eleuthera) as separate islands to the north, which again would place Guanahani quite firmly on San Salvador.

How can a scholar with any credentials in marine geography come up with a finding that the landfall island of Guanahani is in fact the small Egg Island off the far north island of Eleuthera (Cigateo), or the farther south Samana Cay (Samana), or still farther south, the islands of Mayaguana (Mayaguana), Caicos (Caycos) or Grand Turk (El Viego). I can answer that very easily. It's because these scholars ignore the geographers and cartographers who preceded them and who had obtained their information from many first hand, valid, and knowledgeable sources. Instead these scholars, with myopic and misguided vision, go through a convoluted and esoteric analysis of Columbus' nebulous log of the inter-island track for an answer they say overrides all other strong evidence to the contrary.

I would submit that the seven maps and charts that I have just reviewed were certainly not made by analyzing Columbus' descriptive words in the inter-island portion of his log! These charts were made from Columbus' chart of the islands (and other pilots who followed him) to present a true picture of geography that is quite unattainable from romanticized verbal descriptions.

In fact a close scrutiny of the entire National Geographic Society argument (and others as well) shows that they have religiously followed this flawed approach to the problem and their argument is filled with bold and seemingly authoritative assertions that have no basis in historical fact. This same statement applies to most of the other scholars involved in this subject who have named the nine different landfall islands. Their research is based primarily on tedious trivia in the log, which they put forth as inviolate navigational data to establish the track and the landfall.

In this chapter I have established the fact that San Salvador is the true landfall by fully meeting the requirements of *all five* of the *essential required criteria*.

While I have limited my negative argument (for the sake of clarity and brevity) to only the Samana Cay contender, this same argument or thesis effectively rules out all the other myriad proposed landfalls north or south or west of San Salvador.

But I would hasten to add that while establishment of the true landfall is an important part of this book, an equal or more important part has been setting the historical record straight in giving a true perspective of Columbus as a man and as a navigator.

It is as a navigator that Columbus made his impact and mark on history. And this mark which had such a profound effect on the history of the world was not made as just any navigator, but as "God's Navigator" to join the Old and the New World in what Columbus visualized as a noble and inspired enterprise.

Epilogue

This book has condensed a mass of detailed historical facts and related technical navigational data into a thesis which shows that many of our past and present historians have painted a picture of Columbus the man, and particularly Columbus the navigator, that is completely false and at odds with true verifiable history. A highly technical book such as this will normally take several readings before all the many significant facts presented will be assimilated into acquired knowledge. In this I would hope to follow a well established rule of communication and save the reader a second reading of the book by presenting a brief review of the more significant conclusions which have been established and documented.

These established and proven conclusions and historical facts follow the chronology of the book rather than any order of importance.

Columbus and his family were well established Genoese citizens and devout followers of the Catholic Faith. The other spurious and conflicting theories that have appeared on the scene have been so thoroughly destroyed by the historical research of Paolo Emilio Taviani that this matter can be firmly put to rest.

Columbus believed that he was Divinely ordained to bring Christianity to the New World and his motives and goals were of the highest order. The fact that these goals were perverted by Europeans who followed his discovery can hardly be blamed on this seaman and navigator who found the route. To do so is like blaming the physician for the cancer.

I have shown that Genoese navigators in the Columbian era were accepted by the European nations as the best trained and experienced ocean navigators available. And in this group of knowledgeable Genoese navigators,

Columbus easily stands out as one of the best (if not the best) of the trained and experienced navigators among his European peers.

Columbus navigated by dead reckoning and he did this with precision and accuracy. His log of the Trans-Atlantic passages reflects this by being an accurate navigator's log that any experienced ocean navigator can follow to establish his track as I have done.

Columbus attempted on several occasions to verify his dead reckoning latitude (quite unsuccessfully) with a sighting of Polaris (the North Star). This and other casual celestial observations has led some scholars to draw unfounded speculative conclusions, out of all proportion to reality, that Columbus was at least a century or two ahead of his time in the application of celestial navigation.

The primary argument against the accuracy of Columbus' dead reckoning navigation and thus the accuracy of his log relies on the premise that the navigational tools he had were so crude and primitive that he could not possibly steer an accurate course or record it accurately in his log. But I have shown (and documented) how Columbus as well as other contemporary navigators of equal skill could have, and in fact did, use these instruments in a constructively accurate manner. This same sort of muddled thinking could be used to prove that the Egyptians could not possibly have built the pyramids with accuracy, or the Romans could not possibly have built their coliseums or aguaducts with accuracy, or the middle age architects could not possibly have constructed their mighty cathedrals with accuracy, because their tools were equally crude and primitive.

I have also shown that the proper and controlled use of a sailing vessel to reconstruct the track of the voyage is far superior to use of a computer programmed with erroneous and flawed data. Every projection of the Columbus track that I have seen is doomed from the very start by the false and unproven control factors used in their manual computation or computer programming. My pragmatic and empirical reconstruction solves this problem in the only way possible by providing the accurate and proven control factors of 15th century magnetic variation and then most importantly, letting the actual currents (not those from the inadequate pilot charts) correct the preceived and reported track to the actual and true over the bottom track made good.

In Chapter 7, I have presented a fresh new approach to solving the enigma concerning which of the many proposed islands is the true landfall of Columbus. This new approach only follows the well established rules of jurisprudence in considering all five of the witnesses (criteria) instead of relying on only one or two of the weakest. Then this new approach quite firmly establishes San Salvador (Watling Island) as the true landfall in the New World.

The Phileas Society in 1989 and the U.S. Naval Institute in 1992 conducted seminars in which proponents of several of the proposed landfall islands were given a forum to debate their several theories. While not meaning to impugn the intended worth of these seminars, they both degenerated into a convoluted and meaningless re-hash of the endless trivia contained in the romanticized description of the islands Columbus encountered after his landfall on Guanahani. Unfortunately in these and other written debates of the subject, the participants have become so engrossed in determining the exact height and circumference of a particular tree and the exact color and texture of the leaves, that they haven't been able to see the forest which surrounds them.

If only Columbus could have attended these seminars I'm sure he would have said something like this:

"Gentlemen, I wrote that description of the islands to show Ferdinand and Isabela what the Indies looked like! If you want to know exactly where I went through the islands after landfall then just consult my separate chart of the islands. And if you want to further locate Guanahani on your charts then consult my accurate navigation log of the over-water passage from Gomera. But let me caution you that my log will show my landfall only in relation to Gomera as I was unsure of my latitude and longitude, so you will just have to figure that one out from my log."

In this book I have done just what Columbus advises here. We don't have Columbus' chart of the islands but in Chapter 7, I have analyzed seven subsequent charts that were based on his chart (and others that followed) and like he said, I can easily identify San Salvador as his landfall island of Guanahani.

Then in Chapters 5 & 6, I again took Columbus' advice and reconstructed his track from Gomera using his log and again determined that his landfall was San Salvador. Unlike Columbus I can even give the correct latitude and longitude for his landfall.

In the history of the landfall controversy, each new proposed landfall (no matter how bizarre) has held center stage for a while and obtained some following in the academic community until bumped off by the next island in line. As I have stated, the latest island with any degree of acceptance is Samana Cay as proposed by the National Geographic Society. Even though I have shown rather conclusively that the National Geographic Society is wrong in this instance, they are going to be difficult to dislodge because of their high standing among their some 800,000 members (of which I am one).

While I have limited my argument to just the two leading contenders for the landfall (San Salvador and Samana Cay) we cannot totally ignore the many other islands, so to be fair we must choose from this hodge-podge of islands we are faced with. How can we obtain some order from this seemingly chaotic confusion?

Surely by now we have enough viable and consummated research in this over-all matter for an impartial judge or jury to listen to the witnesses, consider the facts, and rule on the multi faceted verdict which includes the true picture of Columbus' intrinsic character, his expertise as a navignator, the accuracy of his log, and his true landfall in the New World. But where are we going to find this impartial judge and jury? I have despaired of an academic seminar or academic blue ribbon committee to render an honest and unbiased verdict as they are too close to the problem.

That is the primary reason I have enlarged my academic papers and written this book for the general reading public.

You, the many readers, are the impartial judge and jury I have been seeking. I have complete faith that you can take the facts documented in this book and wading through the controversy, see clearly the true picture of the life and voyages of Cristoforo Colombo, God's navigator.

Bibliography

This is a selected bibliography containing only the most important references. Technical publications pertaining to ocean navigation are omitted for obvious reasons. Authors mentioned in the text are in some instances contained in extracts from this list.

Bradford, Ernle - *Christopher Columbus.* The Viking Press, New York, 1973.

Bass, George F. - *A History of Seafaring.* Thames and Hudson Ltd., London, 1972.

Becher, A. B. - *The Landfall of Columbus on His First Voyage to America.* J. D. Potter Lmt., London, 1856.

Brigham, Kay - *Christopher Columbus*, His Life and Discoveries in the Light of His Prophecies. Libros Clie, Barcelona, Spain, 1990.

Brown, Lloyd A. - *The Story of Maps*, Little Brown & Company, Boston, 1949.

Burckhardt, Jacob - *The Civilization of the Renaissance in Italy.* Random House, Inc., New York, 1954.

Carpentier, Alejo - *The Harp and the Shadow*, (Translated by Thomas Christensen) Mercury House Inc., San Francisco, 1990.

Casas, Bartolome de Las - *History of the Indies.* (Translated by Andre Collard) Harper & Row, New York, 1971.

Casas, Bartolome de Las - *The Devastation of the Indies.* "Apologetica Historia" (1530), translated by Hera Briffault, Seabury Books, New York, 1974.

Castleman, Bruce A. (Cmdr. USN) - Navigators in the 1490's, *U.S. Naval Institute Proceedings*, December 1992, pp 39-43.

Cline, Duane A. - *Navigation in the Age of Discovery*, International Marine (McGraw-Hill), Camden, Maine, 1990.

Cohen, J. M. - The Four Voyages of Christopher Columbus, from the biography of Columbus by his son Ferdinand. Cresset Library Ltd., London, 1969.

Conti, Simonetta - *Bibliografia Colombiana*, 1793-1990, Casa di Risparmio, Genoa, 1990.

Dunn, Oliver C. and James E. Kelley Jr. - *The Diario of Christopher Columbus's First Voyage to America.* Oklahoma University Press, Norman, Oklahoma, 1989.

Farina, Luciano F. and Robert W. Tolf - *Columbus Documents: Summaries of Documents in Genoa.* Omnigraphics Inc., Detroit, 1992.

Farina, Luciano F. and Marc A. Beckwith - *Christopher Columbus' Journal,* English Edition of the Nuova Raccolta Colombiana, Introduction and Notes by Paolo Emilio Taviani and Consuelo Varela, Ministry of Cultural Assets, Rome, 1990.

Farina, Luciano F. and Gioacchino Triolo - *Christopher Columbus' Discoveries in the Testimonials of Diego Alvarez Chanca and Andres Bernaldez,* English Edition of the Nuova Raccolta Colombiana, Ministry of Cultural Assets, Rome, 1992.

Fox, Gustavus V. - An Attempt to Solve the Problem of the First Landing Place of Columbus in the New World. *Report of the Superintendent of the U.S. Coast and Geodetic Survey,* Appendix 18, pp 346-417, Washington D.C., 1880.

Fuson, Robert H. - *The Log of Christopher Columbus.* International Marine Publishing Company, Camden, ME, 1987.

Gainer, Kim Dian. - The Cartographic Evidence for the Columbus Landfall, *Terrae Incognitae,* Wayne State University Press, Vol. XX, pp 43-68, 1988.

Gerace, Donald T. - *Proceedings, First San Salvador Conference.* College Center of the Finger Lakes, Bahamian Field Station, Ft. Lauderdale, 1986.

Gerace Donald T. - *The Geology of Columbus' Landfall: A Field Guide to the Holocene Geology of San Salvador, Bahamas.* Geological Society of America, Cincinnati, Ohio, 1992.

Gerace Donald T. - *Guidebook for the 6th Symposium on the Geology of The Bahamas.* Bahamian Field Station, San Salvador, 1992.

Granberry, Julian - Lucayan Toponyms. *Journal of the Bahamas Historical Society,* Vol. 13, #1, pp 3-12, October, 1991.

Granzotto, Gianni - *Christopher Columbus*–the Dream and the Obsession (translated by Stephen Sartarelli). Doubleday & Company, Inc., New York, 1985.

Goldsmith, R. A. and P. L. Richardson - *Numerical Simulations of Columbus' Atlantic Crossings.* Woods Hole Oceanographic Institution, Woods Hole, 1990.

Harrisse, Henry - *The Discovery of North America.* Amsterdam, 1969.

Henige, David - *In Search of Columbus.* University of Arizona Press, Tucson, 1991.

Herrera, Antonio de - *Historia General de Los Hechos de Los Castellanos.* Madrid 1601-1615. (see Kelley, J. E. Jr.)

Jane, Cecil - *The Journal of Christopher Columbus,* (edited and revised by L. A. Vigneras). Bramhall House, New York, 1960.

Judge, Joseph - Our Search for the True Columbus Landfall. *National Geographic* magazine, Vol. 170, #5, Washington DC., Nov., 1986.

Keegan, William F. - The Development and Extinction of Lucayan Society. *Terrae Incognitae,* Vol. XXIV, pp 43-53, Wayne State University Press, 1992.

Keegan, William F. - *The People Who Discovered Columbus* - The Prehistory of the Bahamas, University Press of Florida, Gainsville, 1992.

Keen, Benjamin - *The Life of the Admiral Christopher Columbus by His Son Ferdinand.* Rutgers University Press, New Brunswick, 1959.

Kelley, James E. Jr. - In the wake of Columbus on a Portolan Chart. *Terrae Incognitae*, Wayne State University Press, 1983.

Kelley, James E. Jr. - The Navigation of Columbus on His First Voyage to America. *Proceedings of the First San Salvador Conference*, College Center of the Finger Lakes, Bahamian Station, Ft. Lauderdale, 1986.

Kelley, James E. Jr. - The Map of the Bahamas Implied by Chaves' Derrotero. *Imago Mundi*, Vol. 42, pp 26-49, 1989.

Kelley, James E. Jr. - Juan Ponce de León's Discovery of Florida: Herrera's Narrative Revisited, *Revista de Historia de America*, Vol. III, pp 31-65, 1992.

Kelley, James E. Jr. - Estimates of Magnetic Variation Along Columbus' Route on His Second Voyage (Working Notes-MAGVARI) and Postulated 1513 Magnetic Variation in the Bahamas, Personal Communication, Melrose Park, PA., 1988, 1990.

Lamb, Ursula - *A Navigator's Universe*–The Libro de Cosmographia of 1538 by Pedro de Medina. Translated and Introduction by Ursula Lamb, University of Chicago Press, Chicago, 1972.

Lamb, Ursula - Science by Litigation: A Cosmographic Feud, *Terrae Incognitae*, Vol I, pp 43-54, 1969.

Las Casas, Bartolome de - (see Casas)

Lemos, William - Quest for the Santa Maria, A study of construction and performance of 15th century "Nao" type vessels. *Proceedings*, U.S. Naval Institute, pp 109-112, Annapolis, April, 1992.

Lyon, Eugene. - A 15th Century Look at "Niña", *National Geographic* magazine, Vol. 170, #5, pp 601-605, 1986.

MacLeish, W. H. - *The Gulf Stream*. Houghton Mifflin Co., New York, 1989.

Major, R. H. - *Christopher Columbus: Four Voyages to the New World*, Letters and Selected Documents. Corinth Books, New York, 1961.

Marcus G. J. - *The Conquest of the North Atlantic*. Oxford University Press, New York, 1981.

Marden, Luis. - Navigation of the Atlantic Passage, A Columbus Casebook, *National Geographic* magazine, 1986.

Marsden, William - *The Travels of Marco Polo the Venetian*.(translated and edited by W. Marsden and T. Wright). Doubleday and Company Inc., New York 1948.

Martinez Hidalgo y Teran, J. M. - *Columbus' Ships*. Edited by H. I. Chapelle, Barre Publishers, Barre, Mass., 1966.

McElroy, John W. - The Ocean Navigation of Columbus on His First Voyage. *American Neptune*, Vol. 1, pp 209-240, Washington DC, 1941.

McGuirk, Donald L. Jr. - The Juan de la Cosa Theory of Columbus' First Landfall. Paper presented to the Society for the History of Discoveries, annual meeting, University of Minnesota, October. 1989.

McIntosh, Gregory C. - Martín Alonzo Pinzón's Discovery of Babueca and the Identity of Guanahani, *Terrae Incognitae*, Vol. XXIV, pp 79-100, Wyne State University Press, 1992.

McIntosh, Gregory C. - Christopher Columbus and the Piri Reis Map of 1513, *The American Neptune*, Vol 53, No. 4, pp 280-294, 1993.

Medina, Pedro de (see Lamb, Ursula)

Milanich, Jerald T. and Susan Milbrath - *First Encounters*, Spanish Explorations in the Caribbean and the United States, 1492-1570. Univ. Press of Florida, Gainsville FL., 1991.

Morison, Samuel Eliot. - *Admiral of the Ocean Sea*. Little Brown & Company, New York, 1942.

Morison, Samuel Eliot - *Journals and Other Documents on the Life and Voyages of Christopher Columbus*. The Heritage Press, New York, 1963.

Morison, Samuel Eliot. - *The European Discovery of America, the Northern Voyages*. Oxford University Press, New York, 1971.

Morison, Samuel Eliot. - *The European Discovery of America, the Southern Voyages*. Oxford University Press, New York, 1974.

Murdock, J. B. - The Cruise of Columbus in the Bahamas, 1492.The *Proceedings* of the U.S. Naval Institute, pp 449-486, Annapolis, 1884.

Parker, John - The Columbus Landfall Problem: A Historical Perspective. *Terrae Incognitae*, Vol. 15, pp 1-28, 1983.

Parker, John - *In the Wake of Columbus: Islands and Controversy*. Wayne State University Press, Detroit, 1985.

Pastor, Xavier - *The Ships of Christopher Columbus*, Naval Institute, Annapolis,1992.

Peck, Douglas T. - Reconstruction and Analysis of the 1492 Columbus Log, abridged serial form, five issues, *Encounter 92*, Vol. 3, #4 - Vol. 4, #4, Nassau, Bahamas, 1989-1990.

Peck, Douglas T. - Ricostruzione e Analisi del Diario di Colombo del 1492, *Columbus 92*, Vol. 7, #4, pp 19-24, Genoa, Italy, 1991.

Peck, Douglas T. - "Gooney Bird" seeks Columbus Landfall. *South Florida History* magazine, Vol. 20, #2, pp 5-9, Miami, Florida, 1992.

Peck, Douglas T. - Re-thinking the Columbus Landfall Problem. Privately published essay presented to the "Society for the History of Discoveries," Miami, 1992.

Peck, Douglas T. - Reconstruction and Analysis of the 1513 Discovery Voyage of Juan Ponce de León. *The Florida Historical Quarterly*, Vol. LXXI, #2, pp 133-154, Tampa, Florida, 1992.

Peck, Douglas T. - *Ponce de León and the Discovery of Florida*. Pogo Press Inc., St. Paul, MN., 1993.

Polo, Marco - (see Marsden)

Portinaro, Pierluigi and Franco Knirsch - *The Cartography of North America–1500-1800*. Facts on File, Inc. New York, 1987.

Prescott, William Hickling - *The Rise and Decline of the Spanish Empire*. Dorset Press, New York, 1990.

Provost, Foster - *Columbus*: An Annotated Guide to the Scholarship of His Life and Writings, 1750-1988. Omnigraphics Inc., Detroit, 1990.

Provost, Foster - *Columbus Dictionary*. Omnigraphics, Inc., Detroit, 1991.

Rotz, Jean - *The Boke of Idrography*, containing his treatise on magnetic variation. Published in 1542, edited copy by Dr. Helen Wallis, Oxford, 1981.

Sale, Kirkpatrick - *The Conquest of Paradise*: Christopher Columbus and the Columbian Legacy. Knopf, New York, 1990.

Schott, C. A. - An Inquiry Into the Variation of the Compass at the Time of the Landfall of Columbus in 1492. *U.S. Coast and Geodetic Survey*, Washington DC., 1880.

Scisco, L. D. - The Track of Ponce de León in 1513. *Bulletin of the American Geographical Society*, Vol. 45, pp 721-735, 1913.

Sealey, Neil E. - An Examination of the Geography of Three Major Contenders for Columbus's First Landfall in 1492, *Terrae Incognitae*, Vol. XXIII, pp 39-50, 1991.

Sealey, Neil E. - The Significance of the Geography of the Bahamas in Reconstructing Columbus' route in 1492. *Carribbean Geography*, Vol. 3, No. 1, March, 1991.

Sealey, Neil - Ponce de León's Voyage in 1513 Points to San Salvador as Landfall of Columbus in 1492. *Encounter 92*, Vol. 3, #3, pp 4-5, Nassau, Bahamas, 1989.

Taylor, E. G. R. - Hudson's Strait and the Oblique Meridian. *Imago Mundi*, Vol. III, pp 48-52, London, 1939.

Taylor, E. G. R. - *The Haven Finding Art*. Hollis & Carter, London, 1956.

Taviani, Paolo Emilio - *I Viaggi di Colombo, La Grande Scoperta*. (two volumes) Istituto Geografico de Agostini, Genoa, Italy, 1984.

Taviani, Paolo Emilio - *Christopher Columbus, The Grand Design*. (translated and abridged by L. F. Farina) Orbis Publishing Lmt., London, 1985.

Taviani, Paolo Emilio - *Columbus–The Great Adventure*, His Life, His Times, and His Voyages, (translated by L. F. Farina and M. A. Beckwith) Orion Books, New York, 1991.

Taviani, Paolo Emilio and Consuela Varela (see Farina, Luciano F. and Marc A. Beckwith)

Taviani, Paolo Emilio - *Cristoforo Columbo–Genius of the Sea*, English edition, primarily defining Columbus' family and heritage from Genoa. Ministero per i Beni Culturalie Ambientali, Rome, 1990.

Van Bemmelen, W. - *Observations of the Royal Magnetical and Meteorological Observatory*, Observatory. Batavia, 1899.

Varela, Consuela (see Farina, Luciano F. and M.A. Beckwith)

Wallis, Helen - (see Rotz)

West, Delno C. and August Kling - *The Libro de las profecias of Christopher Columbus*. Translation and commentary of Columbus' "Book of Prophecies". University of Florida Press, Gainsville, 1991.

Wilford, John Noble - *The Mapmakers*. Knopf, New York, 1981.

Winter, Heinrich - The Pseudo-Labrador and the Oblique Meridian. Imago Mundi, MCMXXXVII, pp 61-73, London, 1937.

Winter, Heinrich - The True Position of Hermann Wagner in the Controversy of the Compass Chart. *Imago Mundi*, MCMXLVIII, pp 21-26, Stockholm, 1939.

List of
Illustrations

All Drawings and charts are by the author
except those noted in the credit line

Index